Marketing from the Heart

A Guide to Cause Related Marketing for the Small Business

Peggy Linial

MORPHEUS PUBLICATIONS
SCOTTSDALE, AZ

Scottsdale, AZ

Marketing From the Heart:

A Guide to Cause Related Marketing for the Small Business

By Peggy Linial

© 2003, Peggy Linial

Published by:
Morpheus Publications, LLC
4430 N. Civic Ct. Plaza, Suite 201
Scottsdale, Arizona 85251
888-207-2454

Printed by Bang Printing, Brainerd, Minnesota
  www.bangprinting.com

Senior Editor: Lindsay Stoms

Copy Editor: Susan D. Carville

Cover Design: Vincent Stavrowsky

Interior Layout by TLC Graphics, © 2002, www.TLCGraphics.com

Editorial Assistant: Jessica Zimmerer

ISBN 0-9712486-1-3

LCCN 2002112159

The findings, interpretations and conclusions expressed in this book are entirely those of the author. The author has used all reasonable care to insure that information in this book is correct and accurate and assumes no responsibilities for errors. It is further suggested that before beginning any cause-related marketing campaign you first check with both your attorney and accountant.

Morpheus Publications, LLC

We make a living by what we get.

We make a life by what we give.

— WINSTON CHURCHILL —

ACKNOWLEDGEMENTS

Although the author's name appears on the cover of a book and they accept any credit for its success, the reality is that no book ever comes to life without many people working tirelessly on it. There are several I would like to single out.

First, of course there is my publisher, Chris Cosmas. Without Chris there would be no book, so I am grateful. But more than that, I am grateful to Chris for his constant friendship.

Lindsay Stoms, my editor and great friend, is the opposite of my excitability in that she remains a constant calm. It is only because of her that this book is, in fact, a book and not a variety of rambling documents. It is my hope that Lindsay and I work on many more projects together.

Vincent Stavrowsky, our cover designer, who was always kind and accommodating when we would say, "This is the perfect design...if you could just tweak this or that. And, by the way, could you do this as well?" In the end, he captured in a picture exactly what we expressed in words. What a gift he has.

To Jessica Zimmerer, our editorial assistant, and Susan Carville, our copy editor—thank you so much for all you did.

To Tami Dever of TLC Graphics, without whose talent and patience this book would have never come to fruition.

Theresa Stachowiak, who took the time to create the Web site for this book, with virtually no help from me. Thank you for your patience, but mostly your laughter when I was unglued.

To the following very busy individuals who took the time to speak with me at length offering wisdom, ideas, and suggestions: Dr. James Austin, Author and Chair, Harvard's Initiative on Social Enterprise; Lisa Hammond, President, Femail Creations; Gary Hirshberg, CEO, Stonyfield Farm; David McKee, COO, ALSAC (fundraising arm of St. Jude Children's Research Hospital; Dave Hamby, Dave Hamby Insurance Agency; Margaret Holt, Editor, *Chicago Tribune*; Andy Marks, Editor; *Round Rock Leader*; Stan Huskey, Editor, *The Times Herald*; Rich Rusforth, Station Manager, radio station 102.5; Steve Allan, Program Manager, radio stations WASH and WBIG; Tony Bonilla, Assistant News Director, KTVU television; Pat Tanaka, Assistant News Director, KEYE television; and Nancy Clark, Deputy Editor, *Family Circle Magazine*.

A special thank you to Azriela Jaffe, well-known columnist and author, and Louis Beccaria, PhD, President, Phoenixville Community Health Foundation, for their support.

Thank you also to those businesses committed to helping nonprofit organizations and to the customers who support them. You help someone everyday, perhaps without even being aware of it.

A sincere thank you must go to all of the wonderful people who commit their lives to working with nonprofit organizations in order to make the world a better place for all of us.

To all of those friends who have been listening to me yap about every stage of this book for well over a year, and yet still always ask how it's going. My deepest thanks.

Finally, my love to George, my husband and friend, who would read and reread every chapter without saying, "Didn't I just read this yesterday and the day before?" I would be completely unable to do this without him. He is my greatest support. And, of course how could a book be written without Sammi and Misha, my two golden retrievers, lying under the desk keeping my feet warm throughout it all!

If I have forgotten anyone please accept my apologies and know that I appreciate you.

Peggy

TRICKLE UP PROGRAM

A portion of the profits from this book will be donated to the Trickle Up Program.

This organization was chosen because its focus is the start up of small businesses in the United States and internationally. I don't recall how I came to be introduced to the Trickle Up Program, but I was quite impressed with their mission. After checking them out thoroughly, we decided they were a perfect fit for our book.

Trickle Up was founded by Mildred and Glen Leet in 1979 when they traveled to a Caribbean Island and used $1,000 of their own money to help with the start of 10 businesses. Today, Trickle Up gives micro grants ($100 internationally, $700 in the US) along with business training to those impoverished who wish to start their own business. Applicants must also submit a business plan and have it approved, a minimum number of hours must be worked within the first three months, at least twenty percent of profits must be reinvested or saved, and they must continue to report on their business.

Reports in 2001 show that ninety-one percent of the businesses were continuing after one year and seventy-eight percent have actually expanded. Over 10,000 businesses were started in 2001 thanks to Trickle Up.

An additional fact that made Trickle Up the best choice for our book is the fact that in 2001 a full eighty-five percent of funds went directly to program services with administration absorbing only fifteen percent of funds.

If you would like more information on Trickle Up contact them at 104 W. 27ᵗʰ St., 12ᵗʰ Floor; New York, NY 10001; 212-255-9980; info@trickleup.org or www.trickleup.org.

As the purchaser of this book you have made a contribution towards helping someone take a step out of poverty. Both Morpheus Publications, LLC and Trickle Up thank you!

PREFACE

There are many terms thrown about today describing various types of marketing—network marketing, service excellence, and, recently, cause-related marketing. If you took a marketing class ten years ago, you probably didn't study any of these.

Cause-related marketing is new and still a bit controversial to some. It is the partnership of a for-profit business and a nonprofit organization and is intended to increase revenue for both parties. There are some nay-sayers who believe that partnering with a charity and advertising this partnership exploits the charity; however, company after company is proving this to be untrue. Nonprofits are thrilled for the opportunity—especially in the current market—to be on the receiving end of such marketing plans. Businesses are pleased because profits are rising, and the public is happy to be helping causes they believe in.

Books on this topic that currently exist focus primarily on large corporations partnering with large, national charities, such as Lee Jeans and the Susan G. Komen Breast Cancer Foundation and The Body Shop and the National Coalition Against Domestic Violence. I think it's even more vital for small businesses to partner with small, community charities.

Throughout this book you will discover easy, step-by-step ways to choose a charity to work with, investigate the charity, approach the media, come up with some creative joint endeavors, and much more. You will read examples of how other small businesses have succeeded using cause-related marketing. In the appendix, among other things, you will find listings for the state agencies that govern nonprofits in each state, contact information to check potential charities and their giving records, and sample press releases. Throughout the book you will see profiles of businesses that have utilized cause-related marketing programs.

What possessed me to write this book, you ask? I worked for many years in healthcare, as a hospital department head. In that capacity, I ran a patient support group that became one of the largest in the country. Much of that was attributed to great press and partnerships. I was utilizing cause-related marketing but didn't even know it at the time. It was just common sense to me—get publicity and credit anyone who helps you.

I then worked for many years in medical textbook publishing. When we had books with damaged covers that we couldn't sell, rather than throw them away, we donated them to organizations that couldn't afford new ones. Word got around and people loved us.

When my husband and I moved to Pennsylvania, I decided to open a business of my own. I was tired of the amount of travel required in publishing and had spent my entire adult life in healthcare. I wanted to be a part of my community and do something fun!

Since I had done ceramics since high school, I decided to open a studio where people could paint their own pottery and make their own silver jewelry. There were no contemporary ceramics studios in our area at the time, so it seemed like a great idea. Unfortunately, we lived in a town of about 16,000, and all of the information I had gathered suggested that for success you needed to be in an area of at least 100,000.

Being a bit of a rule breaker, I decided that, in fact, because our town was so small, it really needed an activity-based retail business. So I opened Ceramics by ME, Inc., a place where customers could relax and nurture their creativity. It was also a place for children and adults to have fun; we hosted frequent birthday parties, bridal showers, and family gatherings.

I quickly discovered that whenever our business had coverage in our local paper, we were inundated with business. I also believed that I was very lucky to be living this dream and needed to give back. I was fortunate to be part of a business with a pricing system that is part service and part retail; it provided me with the ability to be creative in my cause-related marketing ventures.

I'll be sharing some of the various projects we did throughout the book, so I won't bore you with details now. What I will tell you is that I discovered quickly that, as word got out about many of our projects, we were contacted by local and national media. I then began to seek it out as well when we were involved in charitable events with our nonprofit partners. All of our exposure led to increased business and loyalty from our already established customer base since they were aware of our contributions and had an opportunity to help others when they supported us.

I frequently was asked by other businesses in our community and surrounding areas, "How did you get channel X to come and film you?" or "How did you get in the paper again?" I would always tell those businesses about what we were doing and occasionally make a suggestion of charity events coming up or worthwhile charities that would love their support. It always amazed me when I received the responses, "Our policy is we don't donate anything," or "I'm a small business, I can't afford to give anything away."

My feeling was just the opposite; as a small business, I could never afford to buy the amount of time we were on television, nor could I afford to buy the amount of white space we received in various newspapers and magazines. Plus, how could I possibly expect a community to support my business when I didn't support the community?

I believe you reap what you sow. Others believe that giving is good karma. Still others believe that what goes around comes around. While these are the morals that I try to live by, I'm not purely altruistic, nor am I trying to spout Pollyanna beliefs. Beyond all of this, I can assure you that a well thought out, strategically planned cause-related marketing campaign is, frankly, just damn good business!

I hope that you will find this book helpful and that you'll visit my Web site www.marketingfromtheheart.com. Please share your tried and true cause-related marketing stories as well as those that didn't work. Feel free to let us know additional sites that you find helpful or charities that you have found worthwhile.

Wishing you much success in all of your endeavors!

Peggy Linial

CONTENTS

FOREWORD

We are trained from our first business school courses to think of the world of business as a one-up, one-down arena. There are clear winners and losers, and the name of the game is to beat out the competitor. Altruism and being kind to customers and treating employees well are all useful endeavors, but for what purpose? To increase profits. Research has proven time and again: treat the people well, and you will prosper. We are shaped as business professionals to be driven by the need and desire to prosper, at the expense, if need be, of other entrepreneurs fighting for the same real estate, the same customer dollars, the same right to say, "We're the best."

And, so it should be. Let's not be Pollyannish about this. Business is tough. Without a competitive edge, you can be out of business in a year. Without employees who are honest and dedicated, and a product or price that is superior, the fickle customer will soon move on and you'll be left with an inventory and a dream, and a whopping mortgage you can't pay. There's nothing wrong with being motivated by the all-American dream to make a buck, to provide for our families, and to enjoy some of the luxuries that living in America affords us.

That's what I appreciate so much about the subject matter of this book: cause-related marketing. It is unapologetic about the profit-driven incentive. It doesn't gloss over it with nice words about why it's so important spiritually and globally for all of us to take care of one another. It doesn't lecture you like a nagging grandmother about why you should be taking better care of those less fortunate, and why you don't really need another Mercedes when there are people starving on the streets. This book applauds prosperity and encourages business owners to achieve it. It also acknowledges that many entrepreneurs *are* inspired by altruism, and that they do feel better about themselves when they tithe a certain amount of their profits towards needy causes. But the book doesn't stop there.

The essence of cause-related marketing is this message: You can profit, while being altruistic. Notice which phrase comes first. It doesn't say, "You should be altruistic, and don't worry, you can make it a tax write off and it'll be good for your business, too." Cause-related marketing makes good business sense. Companies and entrepreneurs engage in these practices because it is profitable! And they can do so unapologetically. Rather than pretending that the *only* reason why a company would lend a hand to a nonprofit or struggling cause is because of altruistic and selflessness, cause-related marketing sets the record straight: This could be one of the best kept secrets and best avenues to prosperity that a small or large business owner could find. And yes, while engaging in this creative way to make a dollar, you do earn big brownie points up in heaven, too.

It's about time we strove for more win-wins in the world of business. If there's a strategy that increases profits, sometimes tenfold, and all the while, it helps the customer, your employees, and the community, why not pursue it with vigor? There are no losers in cause-related marketing. When it works, everyone is a winner.

Who is this book for? You might think it's only for those religious folks who always give to charity, but you would be wrong. Cause-related marketing appeals to any business owner who seeks greater profits, period. And, along the way, by following the principles outlined in this book, you'll be able to help a lot of people, too. Hallelujah! Don't you just love a win-win?

Azriela Jaffe
Syndicated columnist and author of
Create Your Own Luck and *Permission to Prosper*

INTRODUCTION

As a small businessperson, either starting out or already established, you may say to yourself: "My business isn't big enough or profitable enough to participate in the community by giving back. That's for the big corporations! They make the money!" Well, nothing could be further from the truth. Such a statement, pardon the expression, is a cop-out!

While the concept of cause-related marketing has its roots in big business, its practice and influence can and should be spread far and wide to all levels of the business community. The reason that it is such an important practice to cultivate for small businesses as well large businesses is that cause-related marketing is a win-win situation for both sides of the business/fundraising equation.

When a solid nonprofit organization partners with a reputable local small business enterprise that has compatible values and that identifies with the nonprofit's mission, much good can result. While the nonprofit organization can add much needed dollars to its coffers to better serve its clients and pursue its cause, Mr. and Ms. Small Business can sell more product and help others at the same time. As the saying goes, you "can do well while doing good."

It's a well-known business fact that people prefer to do business with an enterprise that has a heart for the community and sees itself as playing a committed civic role. The simple fact is that by patronizing such a business, customers feel better about themselves because they view themselves as giving back at the same time. It's the proverbial "two-fer"—both the business and its customers are uplifted by the process. (And that's a good thing!)

The time spent reading *Marketing From the Heart: A Guide to Cause Related Marketing for the Small Business*, I can guarantee you, will be a great personal investment that you won't regret having made. You will not only gain a deep understanding of what cause-related marketing is and how it works, but you will also become an advocate for its practice and will want to recruit others to follow your lead.

Louis Beccaria, PhD
President and CEO
Phoenixville Community Health Foundation

Marketing from
the Heart

CHAPTER 1

What Is Cause Related Marketing?

Before we begin any discussion, let's define the phrase. In short, cause-related marketing (CRM) is the mutually beneficial partnership of a for-profit organization and a nonprofit organization. If you are just starting your small bed and breakfast, dog walking service, gift shop, or automotive repair business, this concept might sound a bit foreign. Here's how it works:

Your business (the for-profit) provides something for the John Doe Foundation (the nonprofit), and both of you benefit through a financial gain or public awareness, which ultimately translates into financial gain.

You've probably seen large corporations such as Ben and Jerry's and The Body Shop, not to mention the most noted example, American Express, entering into such partnerships. In the last few years, every October, which is Breast Cancer Awareness Month, just about every large fashion designer got on the CRM bandwagon. One company donated a portion of profits made on their line of jeans to the Susan G. Komen Foundation. Another company sold pink ribbon T-shirts to benefit the cause. Even the cosmetics company Avon sold pink ribbon pins to help raise funds for breast cancer research.

Some may view cause-related marketing campaigns as sales ploys that tug at heartstrings and take unfair advantage of our emotions. However, I disagree. My mother-in-law had breast cancer, so I bought Avon's pink ribbons for everyone in the family as well as for another friend of mine who had the disease. Had I gotten sucked in, as many would think? Although I didn't really need the ribbons, I liked the idea of showing solidarity and banding together to raise awareness. Since I knew a portion of the proceeds went to cancer research, I felt I was helping in that way as well. Because of this, I didn't feel that the company had taken advantage of me at all. In fact, I was happy about my purchase and felt good about what Avon was doing.

Did Avon make a profit? Not on that particular item, but they certainly profited from the goodwill and publicity generated by that partnership. It is my opinion that, as a business, they have a duty to give back, and they do. The ribbon pin is not Avon's only breast cancer awareness program. Since 1993, they have raised over $165 million for this cause. Because of their efforts, I would certainly buy from them again, even if a product of theirs were priced a bit higher than another similar product, and I am not alone. According to the 1997 Cone Holiday Trend Tracker, 76% of black consumers and 88% of white consumers factor in a company's charitable reputation throughout the year when they make a purchase.

Consider the number of flags sold after September 11. Most flag companies gave a portion of profits back to the Red Cross or one of the many emergency workers funds, but they also kept a large amount of the money generated by these sales. Personally, I find no fault with that, and neither do most people I know. After all, we needed and wanted those flags to show our support and grief. When buying the flags, people felt as if they were helping in a time when we all felt helpless. In fact, a national poll commissioned by Cone, Inc. and conducted September 21-24, 2001 showed that 62% of Americans feel it is appropriate to tie a percentage of proceeds of a product to supporting victims.

Now that we've seen some examples of what cause-related marketing is and have talked about how some large companies are using it, you are probably left with a huge question: How do I, the small or home business owner, utilize CRM? After all, I have few, if any, employees, and we aren't even in the black yet. James Austin, PhD, chair of Harvard's Initiative on Social Enterprise and author of the book *The Collaboration Challenge: How Nonprofits and Businesses Succeed Through Strategic Alliances*, says, "One of the powerful characteristics of collaboration is that it is not scale dependent. That is, you don't have to be big to enter into a meaningful relationship with a nonprofit organization. Small can be beautiful."

If your situation is similar to that just described, I would say this: you, more than large companies, need to use cause-related marketing! You say you are a small business with a miniscule operating budget and want to know how you can afford to do this. Actually, you can't afford NOT to do this!!

WHAT IS NOT CONSIDERED CRM?

Frequently, small business owners say, "I already do that, and it hasn't helped." They go on to explain that they give donations to charities but have found no financial gain from it. When probed further, a typical example they give is that of a local charity sponsoring a run and their business is asked to donate money and/or supplies. The owners do, whereupon they are graciously thanked and provided a receipt for tax benefits. Or they send a check to the American Cancer Society or make an annual donation to their local library and, again, receive heartfelt thanks. This is usually where the relationship ends.

I applaud and encourage any contributions to worthy organizations. However, I will also tell you that if you contribute with a marketing strategy in mind, it will provide more bang for your buck for both you and the organization that you wish to help. It then becomes a true win-win situation.

MAKING CRM WORK FOR YOU

Considering the previous discussion regarding what constitutes cause-related marketing, let's examine a few hypothetical situations and plan a plausible campaign. John Doe was a child tragically killed in your town. The family started a foundation to raise money and provide scholarships in his name. The foundation sponsors a run, which is embraced by the community. They come to your gift basket business to ask for a donation. As a small, new business, your funds are limited, but, of course, you want to help. You also want some public credit for helping. Here are some ideas that work for everyone.

You could invite the soccer team from John Doe's school to come to your business and put together gift baskets for the winners of the run. Then stop by the local paper and ask them to send a photographer to the gift basket assembly. Don't forget to invite the committee that organized the run; they'll want to be in the photo, too. In fact, they may already have a contact at the paper; if so, ask them to arrange for the photographer.

If this example isn't feasible for your type of business, another idea is to give to the charity a portion of your profits from one day's business. Again, it is important to ask the paper to run a story.

Perhaps you live in Washington, D.C., and you can't imagine ringing up the editor of the *Washington Post* and asking him to send a photographer. You're correct in your thinking. They can't zip out to every single event, no matter how worthy the cause. You will want to approach the editor that covers the news in your particular area. (Sometimes the "Lifestyle" or "Metro" sections feature the stories appropriate for certain towns or districts.) Otherwise, you will have to think of an approach that has a hook they will want to feature. (We will delve into this topic in Chapter 6, Getting Publicity.)

BENEFITS OF CRM

How does all of this help you and/or the John Doe Foundation any more than if you had written a check for a couple hundred dollars? In this case, both of you have gotten publicity. A local paper will generally not print daily stories announcing a charity run but will include a story of a community coming together to help a cause. So the organization has gotten more free publicity than they originally thought, thanks to you. They will get more runners and probably more sponsors.

Your business has also been featured in the paper as a business that is doing good. Trust me, you probably cannot afford to buy that much white space in a paper. This not only tells people what you are doing in the community, it lets many know that you exist! After such stories were in the newspaper or on television, we welcomed countless new customers who lived in town but had no idea we were there or who didn't know exactly what our business was.

By providing the baskets, you have also allowed the public to see your beautiful work in the newspaper and at the run where the baskets will be displayed. You also enlisted the help of a group of children, which gets families into your business to drop them off and pick them up. They will see all you have to offer and will most likely remember you when they are looking for unique teacher gifts!

Beyond all of the benefits mentioned above, the truth is that it probably costs you less to donate several baskets than if you had donated money. Remember, you pay wholesale for the baskets and material, but will get retail credit on your donation. In the public's eye you have donated a prize with a $50 value since they know that's what they would have to pay for it. However, you may have only paid $20 for the materials, so simple math will show that if you have limited cash flow, this is the best way for you to give. Since the run committee would have had to pay retail for the prizes that you donated, they got more as well.

Can you think of a more mutually beneficial situation than that? Best of all, it can be done with any business. It just requires a little creativity to come up with the twist that will work for you.

REAL-LIFE SUCCESS WITH CRM

Now, that was a hypothetical situation to show that any business can participate in an event. Let me describe the actual events on which the example was based. In our small town, there was a run for Dana Marie, a seven-year-old girl who was killed when she was hit by a car. At that time, our business had been open only a year and had very little money. We knew that the whole town would be at the run, so we wanted to be involved. In fact, we wanted to be listed as one of their Angel sponsors, which required a $2,000 donation.

Our budget would not allow for that kind of expense, so we had to be creative. First, we gave them a $200 check. Then we said we would donate 100 tiles for kids to paint at the post-run festivities. We also decided to give each of the 800 runners a coupon for one hour of free studio time. Our total donations so far are:

	Cost (Actual)	Donation Value (Retail)
Cash	$200	$200
100 Tiles	$200 ($2 ea.)	$600 ($6 ea. retail)
800 Coupons	Variable, depending upon use	$4,000
TOTAL	$400 plus labor	$4,800

Since we now had hit the Angel level of sponsorship, our name would be on all of the shirts given to runners and in the flyers distributed throughout the community. But we decided to go one step further. A vendor who printed T-shirts said he would make some for us at a very reasonable cost since it was a charity and we had done business with him before. The shirts said: "Ceramics by ME is running for Dana Marie. Won't you?"

All of the employees at the studio wore them all over town, simultaneously advertising for our business and for the run. We also sold them to our customers with the profit going to the Dana Marie Foundation. This allowed us to donate a bit more to the foundation, but also increased name recognition for us, which is extremely important for a new business. Additionally, it let everyone know that we strived to support our community.

There are, of course, costs that I have not added in, such as paint, use of brushes, glaze, firing time, and electricity, not to mention staff salaries. On the day of the event, all of the staff that went donated their time, so that was not an issue. The labor involved in the preparation and firing of the tiles was done while the staff worked their normal scheduled hours. It was understood with the run committee that the tiles would be ready a week later than usual so that extra staff didn't have to be hired.

Because the tiles were small, we were able to squeeze them into the kiln around other items, so I consider that to be a negligible cost. Paint runs about $20 a bottle, however, there is always a bit at the bottom that can't be squeezed out. We took many of those almost empty bottles and cut the tops off to retrieve the unused paint. These bottles would have otherwise been disposed of, so we didn't add them to our cost.

In the end everyone was happy. After the run, the kids could paint tiles, which cost the foundation nothing. The organization also received coupons for each goody bag that cost them nothing. They were thrilled that our staff wore the T-shirts referring to the walk all over town. The paper featured an article with pictures on the front page explaining our partnership, so the foundation got great advertising. This was after the paper had already run a spot about the race, so it was unlikely that the foundation would have been featured on the front page again. In fact, when I first approached the editor, he said they had done a story already, so unless I could come up with a unique angle they wouldn't run another one. Our active contribution—the kids painting tiles along with the additional T-shirts—was that angle. (It will often be your job to find the angle or hook that makes the newspaper salivate. More on this topic will be discussed in Chapter 6, Getting Publicity.)

Our gain was having our name on the shirts worn by each of the runners, as well as the shirts we had printed on our own. After the tiles were fired, parents had to pick them up at our studio, which got them inside to see what we offered. The coupons had the potential to bring in first-time customers. They also acted as a great tracking device to measure the success of this endeavor. This is always key for optimal use of your gifts. Finally, the picture and article on the cover of the paper was great advertising that we would not have had otherwise.

Until we sold the pottery studio, we continued to work with the Dana Marie Foundation in other creative ways that will be shared throughout this book.

BUSINESS PROFILE

MOTHER EARTH COFFEE COMPANY
140 South Euclid Avenue • Park Ridge, Illinois 60068
847-696-0102
Web site coming soon; alltalk@ameritech.net
Owner: Ellen Heller-Leo • Business: coffee café

Ellen only recently opened her store and did so with a mission—to use her business skills to raise money and awareness for various charities.

After her husband's harrowing illness (he's well now), Ellen became increasingly aware of the need for research dollars as well as political clout to make an impact on various social issues. By owning a business and becoming aggressively involved in philanthropy, Ellen will be able to accomplish her mission and have a positive impact on society.

Not only does she sell coffee drinks, but she also partners with a local pastry shop to provide pastries. She commits to donating ten percent of her profits to a charity each month, and she will also host black tie affairs to raise money.

Ellen has received a tremendous amount of complimentary and well deserved publicity for her good works. She plans to open more locations of Mother Earth Coffee around the country in the near future.

Mother Earth Coffee came to my attention when a friend in Chicago sent me an article about the business.

CHARITY PROFILE

Kelly Anne Dolan Memorial Fund
P.O. Box 556 • Ambler, PA 19002
215-643-0763 • www.kadmf.org • Contact: Peggy Dolan

MISSION: Provides for uninsured costs of care for critically, chronically, or terminally ill children.

The day after their daughter passed away from a rare form of leukemia, Peggy and her late husband Joe started this organization. During the time that their daughter spent in the hospital they saw many children whose families could not afford to visit them due to those uncovered costs such as gas, food, lodging, parking, etc. Many families who lived a distance from the hospital needed to stay home and work in order to maintain insurance coverage for their children.

They also met chronically ill children who needed special equipment, such as ventilators, special formulas, and air conditioners, at home in order to live. Many families were unable to provide these necessities. There were also those families who, after suffering their child's horrible illness and then losing them, could not afford to bury them.

The Dolans decided the perfect way to honor Kelly and give thanks for their ability to provide for her until the end was to provide help for others. The fund is contacted by physicians, nurses, and social workers, and response is almost immediate.

Beyond running this organization Peggy donates her time to serve on various other charitable boards.

CHAPTER 2

Getting Started

You've now decided that cause-related marketing is the way to go, and you're ready to start planning. The first thing you have to do is make a few decisions. Whom would you like to benefit from your efforts? Do you want to limit your CRM to just one organization? Either way works, although I have found that, with a small business, serving more than one organization may have broader benefits, which we'll discuss shortly.

CHOOSING A CAUSE

When making a decision about which causes to support, there are several things to consider. A sample worksheet is included in the Appendix to make things easier. While it may seem like a waste of time to think about these qualities and fill out the accompanying worksheet, having your answers down in black and white will help you define your interests and passions. When you are besieged with funding requests in the future, it will be a reminder of why you chose certain charities in the first place. Ponder the following questions to help you narrow your focus.

What are your interests?

Jot down your interests without thinking in terms of a charity. Do you like the outdoors, love animals, adore children, feel passionate about painting, live to eat at fabulous restaurants? All of these things will help you define potential beneficiaries.

You might ask, "Is she crazy? How can the fact that I love food and going to great restaurants be an opportunity?" Perhaps a charity you would like to support would be one that feeds the homeless with dignity. No matter what your personal interests and hobbies are, you can find a cause where you will be able to utilize them.

What tugs at your heartstrings?

Many people are moved to support something that has touched their lives, but others may not be as comfortable with something that hits so close to home. For instance, Shelly Fabares works tirelessly to benefit Alzheimer's research. My own mother had Alzheimer's disease, but, while I give to the Alzheimer's Association, I prefer to work more closely on other campaigns at this time in my life. Working with Alzheimer's causes is still too emotional for me today.

Perhaps someone close to you had or has autism. That may be something that you feel strongly about. Perhaps, anything related to children tugs at your heart and makes you want to help.

Which single group or cause would you most like to help?

If you were given money with the stipulation that it must be used to make an impact on only one segment of the world, what would that segment be? Ponder this question, jot down some answers, and then put them away for a day or so before reviewing them again. The reality is that, sadly, we cannot help and support every worthy cause that exists. You will have to make the decision to narrow it down to one or a small few.

Now that you've narrowed down your own personal causes, think about your business. Do you cater to a particular sector of the population? Are most of your customers children, moms, working women, men, teachers? Do you provide a service that could benefit an organization's fundraising? Let's look at a scenario.

You know you feel strongly about children's causes, and you want to concentrate on local needs. You're a hairdresser with 90% adult clientele. What could you offer that would help your cause while getting publicity (i.e., profit) for you? Perhaps you could take a Saturday in August (just before school starts) and give $1 per customer to a cause that benefits kids. Or you could offer half-price children's wigs, with styling of course, to those children who have lost their hair from chemotherapy.

Of course, you'll want to be sure that you have teamed with the organization benefiting from your gift to be sure that they are as enthusiastic as you are about the project. You will also want to arrange for newspaper coverage prior to the event as well as a photo during the event. If you are in a smaller area where the paper has a limited staff of photographers, they may happily accept a photo from you.

Don't be afraid to contact television and radio stations as well. Invite them to the event; even offer to do the hair of one of the on-air reporters and donate the entire amount from that to the cause. Who doesn't want to see their favorite reporter get a makeover? Additionally, think of the on-air exposure as the station uses teasers during commercials such as: Tune in tomorrow for the 6 PM news and see anchor Susie's new 'do! They promote for more viewership, but while doing so, they are also offering you the rewards of great exposure.

So, how exactly have you profited? We can be pretty sure that the publicity will bring added business. In order to track which advertising/publicity campaigns work and which do not, you should be asking first time customers how they heard of you. This will provide you information for future planning.

Beyond the great publicity, your customer base has been expanded to include the children who received your services that day. If your staff was good to the children and you are supporting a worthy cause, those kids will most likely return, as will their mothers and siblings. You may also gain new customers through word of mouth. Mothers will mention it to neighbors and coworkers while people working for the organization that benefited will publicly sing your praises.

The other very valuable benefit will be name recognition. Future clientele may not have a need for your services today, but down the road they may. Even if they don't, they may be asked by someone at work, church, or in the neighborhood for salon recommendations.

As a small business, you may find that you would like to assist more local causes. Often they are in need of the most help just by virtue of their size and lack of national recognition. You do want to be mindful of a couple things: first, choose causes you believe in; second, don't jump on every bandwagon that comes along.

In every town, you will frequently see funds set up for a child's medical bills or disaster victims who have lost their housing. If you feel attracted to any of these, then by all means participate. Sadly, you aren't able to help everyone. Time and resources are always going to be sorely limited for the small business, so it is imperative that you use them wisely. James Austin, PhD, chair of Harvard's Initiative on Social Enterprise and author of the book *The Collaboration Challenge: How Nonprofits and Businesses Succeed Through Strategic Alliance*, suggests, "Be careful not to spread yourself too thin. Sometimes your impact will be greater if you concentrate your resources with one or two organizations rather than channeling little amounts to many groups."

If you are calling the paper and TV weekly and notifying customers about your new helpful project, you will begin to water down your efforts. The editors and producers are not going to want to take your calls. Use your media contacts wisely.

I'm certainly not suggesting you not support the local school's cookie drive or a customer's participation in a Bike for MS. In fact, I think you should support those causes when you can. However, it's probably wise to not pull out all the stops for each event. You can advertise in your store and let the organization know that you will match all donations made by customers for the Bike for MS or give a dollar off coupon to anyone buying a box of cookies for the school. If the organizers want to promote you for these small acts of kindness, be grateful and gracious, but don't take the initiative to get a story in the paper on a routine basis.

Lisa Hammond, president of Femail Creations, a catalog featuring unique art and gifts, is an example of the perfect blend of wisely choosing your charity and promoting it. I don't recall how I came to receive my first catalog since it was some time ago, but I do remember noting Lisa's generous spirit. In each of the five catalogs produced each year, Femail Creations features a charity with a specially chosen item. The charity isn't just briefly mentioned in the catalog; a tremendous amount of space is dedicated to it. All of the details about how the charity was founded and what it does are included. The profits from the designated item are then donated to the charity.

When Lisa began her company six years ago, she wanted to provide quality merchandise and, at the same time, make a difference. The causes that she chooses to support are usually those that help women, children, and the environment. Femail Creations carries many items that are handmade by female artists, as well as other items geared towards women and the home. With this in mind, Lisa has chosen such charities as CERF (Craft Emergency Relief Fund), which benefits artists, RAINN (Rape Abuse & Incest National Network), and The Shade Tree, a shelter for women and children, just to name a few. (Visit www.femailcreations.com to find other charities.)

"When a pebble hits the water, it ripples," Lisa told me when we discussed the importance of cause-related marketing. She has seen powerful returns on her commitment to women and generosity to the art community. She has been recognized as Las Vegas Small Business Person of the Year and has been featured in Oprah's *O* magazine in the Make Your Dreams Come True section.

You can see how Lisa incorporated the ideas from the questions highlighted at the beginning of this chapter. First, she established that her interests were art and women's issues. She then said that the needs of women, children, and the environment tugged her heartstrings. Her number one desire, and the mission of her business, was to empower women. Finally, her business caters mostly to women on both the vendor and customer side. As you saw, her choices of charities reflect all of those things.

Lisa also honors requests for donations to many small functions where she does not actively promote her business but allows her good works to speak to a particular group. For example, she might donate gift certificates or merchandise for a school silent auction. Those people at all involved in the school will know about Femail Creations' generosity. If they haven't already purchased items from the catalog, they might do so in the future.

Although your heart will guide you to your charitable choices, your decision needs to be made and executed in a business-like fashion to be successful. Austin says, "Give the community involvement activity the same care and systematic management attention that you would your other business activities. Don't simply consider it a peripheral activity."

It sounds a bit overwhelming when you are just getting started, but over time the decision of whom to support and how to do it will become much easier.

BUSINESS PROFILE

LITTLE FLOWER INN
225 Madison Street • San Antonio, Texas 78204
210-354-3116 • www.littleflowerinn.com
Owners: Christine and Phil Touw
Business: bed and breakfast

After retiring from the Army, the Touws fell in love with a ninety-year-old home in San Antonio. They purchased it and restored it as a beautiful bed and breakfast. Because they believe their life has been blessed, they feel that they must give back.

Each quarter they select one charitable organization and donate ten percent of their profits to it. Their passion is for animals, so they lean towards organizations that support animal-related causes. You may find out about their current charity by visiting their Web site.

Christine says they hear often that a guest has chosen to stay with them because of their support of charitable organizations.

I first became aware of them when searching through a bed and breakfast book. Their charitable gifts made them stand apart from the other establishments that were included in the book.

CHARITY PROFILE

EDUCATIONAL INSTITUTE ON AGING (EIA)
2205 Hancock Dr. • Austin, TX 78756
512-467-2242 • Contact: Donna Loflin

**MISSION: Promotes better understanding of aging and
long-term care in Texas. Involved in research and
legislation to better serve older adults.
Provides educational opportunities about aging to the
general public, organizations, and individuals involved in
housing and services for older adults and the disabled.**

EIA is the foundation arm of the Texas Association of
Homes and Services for the Aging. Each year they sponsor the Art is Ageless art contest and show across the
state to highlight the talents of older adults in long-term
care facilities. The show is on public display for a month
each year. Winners of the show are then showcased in a
calendar of which 100% of the purchase price goes
directly to EIA.

The Educational Institute on Aging is committed to
increasing awareness of issues and working towards solu-
tions that make a better life for older Americans.

CHAPTER 3

Selecting A Beneficiary

One of the hardest decisions you will have to make is deciding what organization or organizations will benefit from your giving. In Chapter 2, you were presented with questions to help determine your interests. No matter what categories you decided upon, you undoubtedly will find many groups that are worthy of your support.

THE COMPANY YOU KEEP

I can't stress enough how important it is to choose wisely. That old adage, "You're known by the company you keep," applies to business as well as other areas of life. If the organization you support winds up in any sort of scandal, you will most likely be attached to it no matter how innocent and altruistic your intentions.

Let's say that you own a small restaurant and you want to hold a fundraiser to benefit a local organization that feeds the hungry. (We'll call this fictional organization FEED.) It's comprised of college students interested in ridding the community of hunger. You've been impressed with the young men and women who have approached you.

You decide to sponsor a dinner, charging $50 per couple, of which fifty percent will go to FEED. You secure the local high school jazz ensemble for entertainment, your staff offers to donate 100 percent of their tips and salary for the night, and you put out a jar to collect money from the patrons. Everyone is so enthusiastic about the dinner that you book all available reservations the day the article appears in the paper. You've even decided to make this a monthly event.

Everyone—the community, your staff and, of course, your patrons—are thrilled to be helping. You've also gained business for your efforts, including catering several important business functions in town. Life is great!

Then it happens. Six months later, the kids have gone on a very luxurious spring break trip to Hawaii. A cracker-jack investigative reporter starts digging. It turns out that FEED is a scam. The group has made small contributions to a couple of local food banks, but most of the donations have gone into their pockets. Charges are filed and a huge investigation ensues. During press conferences, the district attorney identifies various businesses that were taken advantage of, including yours.

Is any of this your fault? Of course not. Your heart was in the right place. Unfortunately, you may be tainted, and the next cause-related marketing venture you try might be questioned—at least for a while. People who support your efforts will expect that you have properly investigated the charity reaping the benefits.

CHECK THEIR RECORDS

Don't let this type of scenario scare you off. Just use some caution when you decide to team with an organization. Don't be afraid to tell someone who approaches you with what sounds like a great cause that you need to look into it first. Louis Beccaria, PhD, an expert in fundraising and president of Phoenixville Community Health Foundation, suggests that you ask for proof of their 501(c)(3). This is an IRS designation that assures they have gone through the appropriate rigorous requirements to be recognized by the IRS as a legitimate nonprofit.

You can also go to the IRS Web site and review the information on charities and nonprofits. Once in their charity section, you can do a search in their Publication 78 for a charity you're thinking of donating to. This is a database of organizations that may receive charitable donations and any restrictions on them. Remember that you will have to enter the charity's name exactly as it is registered.

If for some reason the organization is not found in a search, don't panic or become concerned. There could be several reasons for this:

- they are under an umbrella foundation with a different name;

- another organization is acting as the fiscal agent for a project;

- you typed the name incorrectly; or

- the IRS made a data entry error.

Simply contact the charity and speak with them, explaining the situation. If they are a legitimate organization, they will easily and quickly resolve the situation. They will be glad you brought it to their attention, since it is likely that others are finding the same unsatisfactory information when they search. If their response is at all adversarial, you will have to make a choice: either proceed without the information from the IRS since the cause is so important to you, or move on to another organization.

If you look at the IRS Publication 78 you will be amazed at just how many organizations are in operation. As an example, the IRS has a special list of charities formed to benefit those who suffered in the 9/11 attacks. While browsing through them, I was overwhelmed with the number of organizations. They are listed alphabetically, and I had counted 100 different charities by the time I reached G. This should give you an idea about how many groups are in need of support.

STICKING TO YOUR FOCUS

The small community business will be approached often to donate to everything from a church's silent auction to sponsoring a little league team to placing an ad in a school's spring musical program. It's possible to have twenty or more requests in a month. You will have to decide early on if you want to give to just one cause or a specific category of causes. Recently, I was coordinating a silent auction, and I was in the position of approaching businesses for support. Since the auction was for a state organization, I didn't concentrate on local businesses but rather on chains that had multiple locations, so that anyone in the state could bid on the items. One of the places I approached was Barnes and Noble. I spoke with the community representative and faxed him the appropriate information. I received a very nice letter informing me that, while they wished us well, their policy was to support literacy endeavors only.

On a personal level, I wasn't happy since I spend a couple hundred dollars a month at Barnes and Noble. Frankly I would have been thrilled if they had even donated one of their picture books from their clearance section. I do, however, respect that they have chosen a specific and appropriate cause to support. Literacy charities are clearly a wise match for bookstores.

LOCAL VERSUS NATIONAL CHARITIES

Now that you have narrowed down your potential partners, it's time to decide whether you'll support local or national groups. While a national organization is always more than happy to have your support, you will probably not get adequate attention from the organization or the press. National organizations usually have the support of large corporations and need to allocate their resources to them. Since the donations will most likely be large and publicity will reach a wide audience (i.e., more potential donors), this makes good sense for the charity.

Smaller community organizations tend to need your support more than the national charities. The odds of national billboards popping up advertising that Levi's will donate one dollar from every pair of jeans sold to Star City Children's Home in Star City, Nebraska, are pretty slim. After all, will this persuade customers in Los Angeles or Chicago to purchase jeans? It is likely, however, that consumers in and around Star City will be swayed to purchase from businesses that support their community organizations. The fact that the children's home wants and needs local business support makes them an ideal organization to work with, as they will probably be very accommodating.

My intention isn't to sway you from supporting national organizations. I just want to provide you with some facts to consider when making your choice.

Many large national nonprofits have a dedicated person to run their corporate partnership program. For instance, St. Jude Children's Research Hospital actually has an online application to be a corporate sponsor. I would recommend you go to their Web site at www.stjude.org, click on "ways to help," and review their information. They are a great example of a nonprofit's CRM program.

Remember that if you donate on a national level, you will be competing for limited media focus against large corporate giving with big dollars available for advertising. Since the media attention is imperative to the success of your CRM campaign, you may want to rethink this approach.

Does this mean that if breast cancer awareness is your passion that you should abandon it? Absolutely not— just bring it to a more local level. Contact your local hospital's development office and speak with the director about how you might be able to work together. Be sure to have a written proposal showing how it will benefit them as well. Remember: it's a two-way street. Hospitals today are fighting their own battles and need goodwill in their communities. Partnering with a local business could be just the way to foster local support.

If the hospital isn't willing or able to work with you, try a women's center or even a local family practice or OB/GYN group. You could offer to put up flyers in your business, perhaps offer a free or discounted item or service with a confirmation of a mammogram, host a night of inspiration at your business, including wine and cheese plus a guest speaker or two. You might have a doctor speak on the importance of early detection or new research or maybe even a survivor who attributes her survival to early detection. Give everyone pink ribbons. You might even be able to include your local Avon representative. They also need publicity and, remember, that they sell beautiful pink ribbon pins.

In the previous examples, you have helped in the fight against breast cancer yet you've brought it to a local level and made it press-worthy.

Beccaria points out that, while all nonprofits need contributions, smaller donations will have a bigger impact on smaller community organizations. You may think,

"My business is too small to provide the kind of help that Avon, Nike, or other large companies can. Will what I do really help?" Beccaria encourages business owners to heed the message he has hanging on a plaque in his office, "No one can do everything, but everyone can do something."

If you don't already have a particular organization in mind to benefit from your efforts, ask around. Check with your neighbors, scan your local newspaper, and talk to people at schools and churches. Don't forget your customers—they are often your greatest resources. They'll be happy to share worthy causes they know of.

SINGLE VERSUS MULTIPLE BENEFICIARIES

If you opt to work with several different organizations, you may still want to primarily be aligned with one or two more closely.

For instance, our business felt especially close to the Dana Marie Foundation, a local organization that gave scholarships each year to honor Dana Marie, a 7-year-old who was killed in a tragic accident in our town. Along with the annual run, of which we were one of the sponsors, we made jewelry with their logo design for them throughout the year as an ongoing fundraiser.

We also felt very close to the Kelly Anne Dolan Memorial Fund. This organization was started 25 years ago by Peggy Dolan after her daughter passed away from a rare form of leukemia. The Fund provides for uninsured costs related to a child's illness.

For their organization, we provided all studio revenues for a designated day, made jewelry with their logo design as an ongoing fundraiser, and donated to their silent auction. (A portion of the profits from my first book goes to them as well.)

As a small retail business, we couldn't afford to have any additional ongoing partnership with other organizations for a couple of reasons. First and most obvious, we had limited resources. We also didn't want to spread ourselves too thin. With only a few employees, we couldn't have possibly taken on any more custom logo jewelry. Since each piece was handmade, we would have had to hire an additional artist to handle that workload. We also had to continue accommodating our regular customer base, which couldn't be put on the back burner without losing customers. It is important to know your limits and stick to them.

Both of our primary nonprofit partners met our mission criteria of helping women and children. Fortunately, each of the organizations had very different requirements of us, which allowed us to accommodate both relationships. As I mentioned, the Dana Marie Foundation has one annual run that functions as their main fundraiser. We knew when it was held and we planned accordingly, both in terms of a labor commitment and financial commitment.

On the other hand, the Kelly Anne Dolan Memorial Fund, which is a much larger charity, is very flexible. While they have their silent auction on a particular date, other fundraisers are scheduled for a mutually convenient time for both the fund and the supporting business. This allowed us to be creative and come up with ideas that would benefit both the Dolan Memorial Fund and our own business. It also allowed us to come up with events at a time when publicity was most needed for either the Dolan Memorial Fund or us. Peggy Dolan, the executive director, was always willing to do whatever it took to get a photo or story in the paper for us since it benefited her organization as well.

If each group had its annual fundraiser near the same time, logistics would have required that we choose one organization or the other. It would have been impossible to heavily support two organizations with similar time and resource demands. Also, if the two large events had occurred within the same month, the media was not going to respond as positively as they would if we contacted them in six months intervals. (Remember that the media is one of the key components to a successful campaign.)

While committing to two primary organizations, we were still able to help several smaller groups on a one-time basis. We were frequently contacted for school functions—private schools often hold silent auctions, as do churches and other charities and civic organizations.

The first year or so we were in business, we granted every request that came in the door. If they handed us a request letter, we handed them a check, gift certificate, or item to be auctioned or raffled. It didn't take long to figure out that we weren't going to stay in business very long doing it that way, and once we were out of business we wouldn't be able to help anyone.

According to Gary Hirshberg, CEO, Stonyfield Farm, a yogurt, soy, and ice cream business known for their support of environmental and organic farming causes, it is naïve to believe that philanthropy has no commercial component. As a frequent keynote speaker, Hirshberg explains he once spoke to a group telling them about an available grant. One component, however, was that you must explain how that grant will impact the sales of yogurt in a positive way. When the audience was a bit taken aback, Hershberg went on to explain the philosophy saying, "If you cut the limbs off of an oak tree, there will be nothing left. However, if you simply drop acorns, eventually you will have many more oaks." By using this analogy, Hershberg conveyed that while we all want to give, unless there is a return, we will be forced to cease our giving and then no one will benefit.

Clearly, we needed a way to reduce the number of organizations we supported. We began to keep a file of requests to sort through, obtaining input from the staff and business partners on each proposed activity. Oftentimes, our regular customers notified us of upcoming benefits for organizations they were involved with and asked if we could contribute in some way. We were usually able to accommodate them, although, more often than not, the contribution was tied to a photo op or article.

Occasionally, when our budget wouldn't allow for the requested monetary contribution, we were given the option to provide something else—discount coupons, gift certificates, or merchandise for an auction. Occasionally, groups loved for us to bring tiles or other tiny items for the kids to paint at the event. At benefit dinners, this was a great idea, since it entertained the children and the families had to come to the studio a week later to pick up their items. It also left us with cash flow that writing a $100 or $200 check would not have. This can be done with other businesses as well. A massage therapist may donate a five-minute hand massage. A florist may donate a small centerpiece. The possibilities go on and on.

AVOIDING THE BANDWAGON STIGMA

If you are going to work with a variety of groups, I would only offer one word of caution: make sure it doesn't begin to appear that you align yourself with every cause you possibly can. If people see your photo in the paper each week associated with a different organization, they may begin to doubt your sincerity. Ironically, it may appear that you aren't committed to anything at all. This perception—right or wrong—can be detrimental to your business.

If it's your desire to help as many worthy causes as you possibly can, you will have to put the right spin on it. For instance, when I began my business I wanted to feature one charity a month. So, perhaps, in October we would support an organization that provides coats to children, and in November we would support the local food bank. I added this to my first press release, included it in my newsletter, and posted information about it at the studio. Since we couldn't possibly know of all the worthy causes in our community, we asked our customers to let us know about groups they would like to have us consider. We also asked customers to help us select organizations to support. You can do the same.

Make the first Saturday or Tuesday of every month charity day. Announce the recipient of next month's Charity Tuesday, and explain that sixty percent of the day's net revenues will be donated. If you have a gas station, perhaps you want to take the cost of one gallon of gas for every filled up tank and donate it to your weekly or monthly charity.

When you go about it in this manner, the perception is that you want to give back to your community on a routine basis. Even though you may choose different recipients, it won't appear that you are suddenly jumping on a new bandwagon every few weeks.

I would still recommend that you stay within your charity mission choice. This way the charities you choose will have some unity.

BUSINESS PROFILE

PAINT YOURSELF SILLY
6546 Tanqua Verde #130 • Tucson, Arizona 85715
520-885-4755 • www.paintyourselfsilly.com
Owners: Tonya Davidson and Sharon Dickerson
Business: contemporary ceramics studio

When Tonya and Sharon opened their paint-your-own-pottery-studio in 1996, they believed that they would support the community that supported them. Tonya says, "If you give, it will come back to you tenfold."

They also believed that the schools lacked an extensive arts program, so they act as a destination for school field trips, providing supplies to the classes at wholesale prices. "Studies have proven that children engaged in art think more creatively throughout their lives and do better academically later," they say. They are committed both to children and art so this endeavor made perfect sense to them.

They offer a variety of fundraising ideas on their Web site. I found them while looking at various Web sites while doing research for my business. Their model is worth taking a close look at.

CHARITY PROFILE

CAMP DEL CORAZON
11615 Hesby Street • North Hollywood, CA 91601
818-754-0312 • www.campdelcorazon.org
Contact: Lisa Knight

MISSION: To provide the opportunity for children with heart disease or a history of heart disease to attend camp.

Dr. Kevin Shannon and Lisa Knight, RN, have full time positions running the Pediatric Electrophysiology Service at the UCLA Medical Center, and yet they began this wonderful camp—first in Kevin's office and then Lisa's apartment.

It began after Kevin discovered that a young patient of his was extremely self-conscious about the surgical scar on his chest. He felt that if the patient could see other children in the same situation it would benefit him. There was a camp in another state, but nothing locally. After sharing this story with Lisa they began Camp del Corazon in California.

Camp del Corazon is fully accredited by the American Camping Association. Camp is entirely free for campers. The only expense is getting the children to the site. Camp is held over Labor Day and there are two sessions—one for children below 7th grade and the other for teens.

The camp has three to six cardiologists as well as fifteen to twenty CCU, ICU pediatric nurses on site. They also have a fully equipped cardiac infirmary, Medi-Evac boat, and, if necessary, air evacuation is also available.

Two very important things to know about this non-profit are that 100% of donated funds go directly to the camp and that all of the physicians and nurses donate their time.

CHAPTER 4

Working With the Beneficiary

Now that you've been talking to friends and customers about your goal to work with a charitable organization, you'll probably notice that when you read about an organization with the same philosophy and passion as your own you will remember them.

When choosing among potential charities to benefit from your cause-related marketing program, take note of important information, such as the exact name of the organization (because many have similar names), the executive director or contact person, and the contact information. Before you approach this organization, do some background work to ensure that they are worthy of your support and customers.

Once the word is out about your mission, everyone you know will be telling you about one organization or another. Don't make a hasty decision. Take information from anyone who wants to help, but think your decision through carefully. Hopefully, once you have chosen your charity or charities you will have a long and happy working relationship with them.

In an earlier chapter, we spoke about selecting a beneficiary. Let's take it a step further and explore some details about working with an organization.

DO YOUR HOMEWORK

Before you make any commitment to an organization, investigate it thoroughly. Make sure they are who they say they are and that the money goes where they say it will. Here are some steps you may want to take.

Is your charity who they say they are?

If the local PTA of your child's school is holding a big fundraiser or you are partnering with a local hospital, you can relax more than if an unfamiliar organization approaches you. Fraudulent charities frequently have names similar to legitimate charities. They use "fund" rather than "foundation" for example. You may be familiar with the good works that The Jane Doe *Foundation* does, but if people have done their homework regarding the legitimate foundation, they may be able to slip by with your help. For instance, if they approach you and tell you they are raising money for exactly the same purpose, will you notice that they give you a card that says Jane Doe *Fund*? Perhaps you won't. Sadly, experts at fraud know that.

If you should ever suspect fraud, report it immediately to your state's nonprofit governing agency, usually the Attorney General's office or Secretary of State. (To find out what office in your state regulates nonprofits check the Appendix.) Once you file a written report with the proper authorities, it will be reviewed and investigated.

You may also want to report it to the Better Business Bureau. They have a division dedicated to charities called BBB Wise Giving Alliance based in Norfolk, Virginia. This organization is dedicated to reviewing national and international charities that fall within the IRS code 501(c)(3).

If you are considering partnering with such an organization, check the report that the Alliance has on file. They evaluate on twenty-two specific aspects including financial statements (which will allow you to see how much is actually going to the recipients of the charity and how much is going to administrative costs), fundraising contracts, board members, and sample grant proposals. While they investigate and report findings, they in no way endorse or condemn organizations. You will have to evaluate the information and come to your own conclusion about the worthiness of potential charities. The Alliance also publishes a quarterly magazine—*Better Business Bureau Wise Giving Guide*. This magazine lists national charitable organizations generating the most inquiries.

Keep in mind that not every charity requests a review by the Alliance. If you don't find them listed, this is not necessarily indicative of their worthiness as a charity. In this case, ask them why they are not listed with the BBB. If a large national organization did not belong, I would see that as a red flag. There may be a valid reason for it, but dig a little deeper before you sign on. Again, if they choose not to because of their size and the fact that they only work locally, you will have to measure their merit in other ways.

Where does my contribution go?

Many people think that 100% of their donations go to assist the cause they have donated to. This is rarely the case. It takes a certain amount of money to keep an organization running.

Even those small community charities that are run strictly by volunteers will have administrative costs. They often need to pay for the professional services of an attorney or accountant and, almost always, incidentals like printing of flyers, insurance to cover an event, and even banking charges.

Occasionally, even professional services will be donated. However, any organization will need to invest some portion of its funds in order to continue to operate. Often, the principle will remain invested and the interest earned is used to fund the charitable works.

Obviously, there are times when there is a one-time fundraiser for a particular cause and all of the money would certainly be used after the event. It's not uncommon for a spaghetti dinner to be held with funds going to purchase a wheelchair for a family or a local school choir has the chance to compete in a national competition and has to raise funds for the trip.

When you look at a charity's giving it is important to know what percentage is used for administrative costs. The American Institute of Philanthropy's (AIP's) Charity Rating Guide recommends that sixty percent or more of a charity's funds should go directly to the services. AIP's Web site, www.charitywatch.org, points out that newer charities may require more money to meet administrative and fundraising costs. Check with the BBB Wise Giving Alliance or another watchdog group to see the breakdown of the charity's financial report.

Paperwork

As Louis Beccaria, PhD, president of Phoenixville Community Health Foundation, suggested in Chapter 3, ask the organization for a copy of their 501(c)(3). This is an IRS designation for tax-exempt entities. The organization should be able to provide you with proof of its status. Without a tax-exempt letter from the IRS, you may not be able to use your donation as a tax exemption.

A retailer providing a product (in some states this includes a service) is required to either pay sales tax or prove that the product went to a state tax-exempt authority. This is different than a 501(c)(3) and is issued by the state. Just because an organization is tax exempt does not mean that it is automatically exempt from paying sales tax. Without the proof in writing from the particular charitable organization, you will be responsible for the sales tax.

If you have any questions concerning the appropriate paperwork, contact your accountant before entering into any agreements.

Who is on the Board of Directors?

Are they hands-on and actively involved in the organization or just a name on the letterhead? CEOs of major corporations often sit on the boards of large nonprofits. They serve in a mostly advisory capacity and are frequently chosen for the skills they bring. Think about how thorough and effective a board would be if they included a CEO, a CFO or accountant, an attorney, a marketing executive, and a media contact or two.

How is the charity perceived in the community?

Since your goal is to make this a mutually beneficial partnership, you should consider how your charity is perceived in your particular community. When the community hears about this organization are they more likely to pull out their wallets or walk away?

A worthwhile charity sometimes may support a relatively unpopular cause or even be linked, perhaps unfairly, to a scandal. While this doesn't mean that you should not give, you may want to think it through. Will supporting this charity cause your business any long-term harm? Will you lose customers because of public outrage? You may be wondering: How can giving to a cause hurt me? Think about the following hypothetical examples.

- Your business is located in an extremely conservative area and most of your customers are older, religious, traditional family people. Considering your demographics, hosting an event or partnering with a very

liberal gay activist group may not serve your marketing goals well.

- If your business is in a large hunting area and many
of your customers are hunters, partnering with PETA
may not be your wisest business move. Why would a
hunter want a portion of their money going to an
organization that would like to ban hunting?

- If a scandal had broken concerning embezzlement by
a director of the charity, the public will naturally be
concerned. This might be a wise time to back away
from this particular charity.

Even though you may fully support any one of these
organizations, you may want to consider doing so pri-
vately as opposed to publicly partnering. The same
would be true for political affiliations.

This restraint may sound a bit hypocritical if you truly
believe in the cause. However, years ago when I worked
in medical textbook publishing, an author wanted to
include a procedure, which was a bit controversial.
Editors, authors, and reviewers discussed the potential
merits and ramifications of the inclusion for hours and
had come to no conclusion. Finally, the publisher
stepped in and said, "Our goal is to sell textbooks. We
don't do controversy." This was a great lesson for me.
While I had strong feelings about the situation, the
reality was that we needed to provide a product that
would sell. Occasionally our hearts rule our heads,
which is often not conducive to making good business
decisions. After all, if we don't continue to grow our

business and customer base, we won't be able to help anyone.

GET THOSE RECEIPTS

Be sure to get a receipt from the charity for any donation you make, be it an in-kind donation, product, service, or cash gift. Your invoice will not be good enough for a tax-deductible gift. Check with your accountant to see exactly what he or she requires and be sure to do this prior to your donation.

MAKING THE CONNECTION

Making the connection is something like a dance. Someone has to take the first step and ask the other to dance, and then someone will have to lead. In a great situation, you will learn to move in synch and no one will have his or her feet stepped on! This should be your hope for your relationship with your charity. After you have thoroughly investigated the potential charity and have concluded that it appears to be an ideal partner, you must initiate a conversation.

First, contact the director and determine a good time to meet face to face, since a meeting in person is the best way to start. This eliminates the added distractions of other business, another phone call coming in, or an e-mail popping up during the conversation.

A meeting should also be a bit more relaxed, giving you the time to get to know each other. If you hope for this to be a long-term relationship with a community organ-

ization, establishing familiarity with each other is important. It will allow you to work together more quickly in
the future when an idea of yours or need of the charity
arises. While most fundraising programs will be planned
long in advance, consider the following scenarios where
a good working relationship with a community charity
can help both parties.

A few years ago the Kelly Anne Dolan Memorial Fund
was asked to provide Christmas for a family. Unlike
many organizations that provide just for the children,
the Dolan Memorial Fund believed that the entire
family should share the holiday. They did so by providing gifts for all members of the household. The next
year, more families were identified. In 2000, Peggy
Dolan, executive director had over sixty families in
need. When she mentioned this, I immediately said,
"Great—my business will help," and we worked together on this additional project.

Had Peggy and I not had such a friendly relationship,
this may not have occurred so quickly and easily. There
certainly would have been a more formal arrangement
about who does what and the time frame. However,
since we had worked together and were comfortable
with each other's styles, we were able to make a decision
and agreement instantly.

Additionally, since I had gotten to know Peggy and her
level of commitment to her organization, I knew that if
those sixty families weren't covered she would be dip-
ping into her own wallet. Knowing all of this and having

worked very well with her previously, I felt comfortable going to my Rotary Club and enlisting their help as well.

Several months later, an opportunity came along that allowed Peggy Dolan to lend my business a hand. During the late summer, since families are preparing for kids to return to school and the holiday season is just around the corner, retail business slows. Because of this we wanted to generate some publicity. I called Peggy and asked if she would come into the studio and let us take a photo of her painting a soup bowl. We'd take it to the paper with an article about the Kelly Anne Dolan Memorial Fund and donate 100 percent of the studio fees from the upcoming Saturday to the fund. With Peggy's help, we got the publicity, had a great Saturday, and donated the studio fees to her organization. Incidentally, since we also charge for the materials, we made money as well.

The media coverage also attracted people that may not have been to the studio before. At the same time, coverage about the Kelly Anne Dolan Memorial Fund raised awareness about the organization. In fact, a customer, whose small charity we had previously helped, read the article and stopped by with a fifty-dollar check for the fund. Again, this win-win situation occurred successfully and quickly due to the relationship that was already established between a for-profit and nonprofit.

Another advantage of a symbiotic working relationship is that you can bounce ideas off of each other. While large charities have professional fundraisers to plan and develop their fundraising events months and years in advance, small local charities often are not afforded that luxury.

The ability to share ideas between the for-profit and non-profit has a tremendous value. Each has particular expertise and experience that will benefit the other. Sometimes, since the charity has such a passion about its cause, it may loose some objectivity. For example, the Glasses for Children organization you partner with, is brainstorming for ideas for its first fundraiser, and they decide to hold a run/walk. They may think that everyone will come even if it is held in January in Montana. Who would want to deprive a child from seeing the snow?

As a Montana businessperson, you know from history that your business drops a bit right after the holidays when cash flow is often tighter. You've been thinking about holding a fundraiser of some sort, but you also know that your county has a Christmas run in December and a heart run in February. Both of these fundraisers are well established and you don't want to compete with them, so what do you do?

Partnering with the established fundraiser might be a great answer for all. Perhaps you have a restaurant. Partnering with one of the already planned runs could work for everyone. You could sell hot cocoa and coffee with the profits being split between organizations. You may wonder, why would everyone agree to this?

Let's say that the Heart Run in February has the proceeds going to the local chapter of the American Heart

Association, and they are sponsored by the local running shoe store. Since your restaurant may cater to hundreds of people who have never been in the shoe store, you bring a whole new audience to the run. Equally, the shoe store clients may not be familiar with your restaurant, so you receive greater exposure. The Heart Association gains more exposure not to mention more contributions from the run and your sales. They may also gain some volunteers.

By putting up flyers in your restaurant you may even help save someone's life by introducing them to Heart Association materials explaining risk factors of heart disease. The bottom line is that you have helped a worthy organization by your participation, another local business by exposing your customers to them, and, of course, your own business through greater exposure. How much more of a win-win situation can you ask for?

GETTING TO KNOW EACH OTHER

Serving as each other's ambassadors makes for a successful partnership. Get to know each other and spread the word. If you are a business, know what your charity is about. How did they come to be? Why should someone want to open their wallet to support them? Does someone run them with a passion for the cause, or is the executive director a nonprofit professional? (The director can be both, and neither one is better than the other.)

If one of your customers asks who runs the organization and why, you should have an informed answer. It would be helpful to know that the mom of a child with multiple sclerosis started the custom size wheelchair program. This would certainly speak to the passion and commitment of the director. Or, perhaps the director has many years of experience in nonprofits, and the organization is lucky to have him or her. This also says a lot about the organization that someone so skilled would commit to it.

When we supported a charity, we wrote about it in our monthly newsletter. I always made sure that whenever the media was present, I spoke at length about the charity and gave contact information for them as well as my own business. In return, we frequently gained new customers who had been referred to us by people who worked for the charities.

A great example of a business as a good ambassador is Femail Creations. On its Web site the company has an entire section titled "Community Empower." Under that heading, there is news about the charities being featured in a current catalog along with a list of items that, when purchased, will help that organization. The section also lists former sponsored organizations including their missions and links to their sites. Additionally, Femail Creations has started an award called Women of Courage. A worthy woman who has made a difference is honored monthly on the site.

UNDERSTAND TIME CONSTRAINTS

As a small business owner, you are able to make decisions quickly on your own or after discussing them with your partners. On the other hand, depending on their bylaws, nonprofits may have limited ability to act independently on some ideas. As a result, they will most likely need time to form a partnership, implement a program, or even initiate an event.

They may be able to give the go ahead for a small, local event, but need their board's approval to form a formal partnership. Remember, prior to committing to them you did some background checking. They will want to do the same thing.

If board approval is required for a partnership or even a single event, it could cause delays in proceeding with a planned project. The length of the delay will depend on how frequently they meet and where your item is on their agenda. Be patient and persistent. You might even want to offer to make a presentation to the board about the benefits of the proposed event or even about partnering.

When you are working with very small, newly formed nonprofits, take into consideration that they may have special constraints. If the directors are strictly volunteers, you may be contacting them at their homes where they may also be dealing with carpool arrangements, dinner preparations, and various other activities. Try to respect their needs as well. Ask about convenient times for you to call. Would certain evening hours be preferable for phone contact? Would they rather be contacted via e-mail or fax?

Don't dismiss the idea of working with a smaller start-up merely because of some minor inconveniences. They often become leaders in the nonprofit world. MADD was founded by a woman on a mission after a drunk driver killed her daughter. There are now chapters of this successful nonprofit across the country.

FINALIZING THE DEAL

Once you have come to terms you should put your agreement in writing. Why bother taking the time to do this? Well, frankly, it's just good business.

Everyone is extremely busy and it's easy to misunderstand what your expectations are of each other. If you are planning a simple event that you are providing a service or product for, jot down the necessary information, sign and date it. It doesn't have to be a long formal contract, but it does need to set forth exactly what you will provide and what you expect in return. Everyone will lose if no one contacts the paper because you think the charity is providing all media responsibilities and they are sure you said you'd take care of that. Be sure that both parties sign the agreement and retain a copy. If you are entering a partnership, you will want a more formalized agreement that will set forth each organization's responsibilities and expectations.

David McKee, COO of ALSAC, the fund raising arm of St. Jude Children's Research Hospital, suggests that even the smallest of organizations have a formalized agreement to avoid any misunderstandings down the road. St. Jude, he says, actually has a check–sheet that lists rules and guidelines to allow for a win–win situation.

TIPS FOR NONPROFITS WORKING WITH SMALL BUSINESSES

As we've discussed, a small business and community nonprofit are often the ideal team. Both are full of passion and spirit, which can only rub off on each other. On the downside both are usually extremely busy, often working on all phases of their businesses themselves or with small staffs or volunteers. For this reason, it is extremely important to treat each other as busy professionals.

I can't tell you how many times I have had someone from a prospective charity "stop by" to convince me to donate or work with him or her. Sometimes that's fine, but occasionally I would be involved with a customer or on the phone. There stood, or so I thought, another customer, so I would rush what I was doing only to find that "the customer" was someone wanting a contribution of either time, product, or money. While writing this book, I have heard this story from other business owners again and again.

Avoid making a bad first impression! If you drop by a business and they are clearly busy, come back another time. Call and ask when would be a better time to meet with them. Also, avoid calling them at a particularly busy time of day for their industry. I know the owner of a restaurant who says it's inevitable that at 11 a.m. someone looking for a charitable contribution would contact him by phone or in person. Since 11 a.m. is just before the lunchtime rush, hearing a pitch from a nonprofit is the last thing he wants to do. On the other hand, he welcomes people at 3 p.m.—it's after lunch and before dinner. In fact, he said the late afternoon break from his usual work is nice.

Likewise, if you run into a business with your children in tow, your concentration will be on them rather than the business you hope to work with. Unless you have checked with the business to ask if it's appropriate to bring children along, try your best to schedule a time when you can sit and talk in a relaxed manner, without distractions, for both of you.

If a business has helped you, don't forget to say, "Thank you." I know, this sounds like a no-brainer; but we once gave a hundred tiles to a charity to use for an art activity to keep the children busy. The tiles had a retail value of $400. Believe it or not a member of the event committee actually told me that they ran out during the event and that next time we might want to consider donating more!

Just a simple message of appreciation for a business can help make all the difference. In another instance, we made a very small donation of products and design to a charity that later raved about how much we had done for them. Guess which of these two charities we looked forward to working with again!

Don't always expect the business to donate everything. If you ever have need for a service or product that they can provide, go out of your way to support them. The business will appreciate it and often may give you an unexpected discount or donation. If a café donates muffins to your event, take your family there for an occasional meal.

If you are purchasing anything from your partner business, pay your bills on time! We frequently worked with a charity whose organizers were strictly volunteers. We sold them a product at a discount, which they, in turn, sold at a higher price to raise money. The problem was that we had to finance the operation, which is not easy for a small business! We purchased the materials and paid the staff; yet the charity would pick up the merchandise and promise a check shortly. Because the organization was run by volunteers and not everyone in the organization was authorized to sign a check, it was often a difficult task to find the individual who could actually pay the bill. Often, we found that we were fighting for our money. While we always got paid (there was never a doubt about that) bookkeeping just wasn't a big priority to that organization.

As a charity, you also have every right and duty to research the business and its practices. If they object, it's time to look for a new partner. To investigate a business you can contact the local Better Business Bureau to see if the business has had any complaints lodged and how they responded; inquire around your community regarding the business' reputation.

While you may think this is crazy—why question someone who wants to give your organization much needed money—you don't want people to link you with an unscrupulous business. Suppose an auto repair shop was giving your organization a percentage of proceeds from all oil changes during a month. Later, it's discovered that they charged people but never changed the oil. The next time your charity holds a function some people may hold back, remembering your connection with such a business while forgetting the good work that you do.

If a business does act in an unscrupulous manner, respond quickly. First, contact your attorney before making any public statements. You will want to be sure that any allegations are true before commenting. Next, contact the Better Business Bureau, the district attorney's office, and immediately put out a press release apologizing for any inconvenience this caused, stating that you knew nothing of what happened and that you have severed all ties with the business. If you had a bad experience, don't let it sour you. Most partnerships work out wonderfully.

A PERFECT RELATIONSHIP

Since this is new for both of you, you may occasionally trip over each other's feet. Try not to let this deter you, and keep plugging away.

Of the many I've spoken to, every one of the nonprofit directors and business owners working together in small and large cause-related marketing ventures was positive and enthusiastic about the relationship. They all felt that it was mutually beneficial. Some said it has reaped more benefits than they could have imagined at the start of the partnership.

BUSINESS PROFILE

ISAAC'S RESTAURANT AND DELI
354 North Prince Street • Lancaster, Pennsylvania 17603
717-394-0623 • www.isaacsdeli.com
President: Phil Wenger • Business: restaurant/deli

Isaac's was started by two college friends as a single local deli. Today, there are nineteen Isaac's throughout Pennsylvania. Since the beginning, the company's mission has been to be active in the communities in which their delis are located.

While they participate in many community charitable events, one of their most innovative programs encourages employees to give back to the community. When an employee donates their time to a local charitable organization, they supply Isaac's with the number of hours donated. Isaac's, in turn, pays that charitable organization $3.50 an hour for the employee's altruism. They also participate yearly in a Hospice event in which they make boxed lunches and sell them to Hospice at a fifty percent discount. Hospice then sells them at the retail price and raises money.

According to Wenger they believe Isaac's is a community member, just like an individual resident. Their charitable efforts have resulted in name recognition and support.

Information about Isaac's was forwarded to me when I began this book by a couple of friends who were aware of the company's altruism.

CHARITY PROFILE

SAFEPLACE
P.O. Box 19454 • Austin, TX 78760
512-267-7233 • www.austin-safeplace.org
Contact: Director of Marketing

MISSION: SafePlace exists to end sexual and
domestic violence and abuse. SafePlace helps those hurt
by this violence to heal and empower themselves.

SafePlace provides prevention, intervention, education, and advocacy to the community so that women, children, and men may lead a safe and healthy life.

This great organization began in 1998 when the Center for Battered Women and the Austin Rape Crisis Center joined together. They currently provide an apartment community, an emergency shelter, and even a school and daycare. Most recently SafePlace has even begun a group for men of all ages interested in learning about and taking action against violence against women and families.

SafePlace is a community organization and is not affiliated with other organizations of the same name. I encourage you to visit their Web site, which is quite impressive, and even lists in-kind donation needs, a great help for businesses.

CHAPTER 5

How to Give

When it comes to giving, most of us think of writing a check or opening the till. If you are brand new in business and have already discovered all of those "extra" expenses that surprised you—paper towels, toilet paper, and soap for the customer bathroom, for example—then the idea of writing a check can be overwhelming.

Of course, you still want to give, and we already know it's the smart business decision. What do you do? There are actually several things that can be done.

IN-KIND GIVING

A wonderful gift is one that is "in kind." This is a donation of an item rather than money. Let's say you own a small electronic business. Perhaps you have old models of stereos, TVs, and VCRs. You can't really spare the space in your store for them since the new models are in, but you don't want to clear them out below wholesale cost. A great solution is to donate them.

You might decide to give them to a nursing home for the residents' common space or to a daycare center. Not only would this gift be treasured, but also you have made an in-kind donation. A portion of this will be tax deductible. (Be sure to speak with your accountant before assuming anything.)

Now, don't just stop by the facility one day and drop it off with a handshake. You should also play your hand well and create some publicity.

If it's a senior center, speak with the executive director, offer to host a small party, and suggest that the board of directors be invited. Bring some cookies and punch; maybe a local dance studio would send some children to perform or a dance instructor to dance with the residents. Invite a Brownie troop or Cub Scout troop to serve the food; they are always looking for community service projects. Don't forget to contact the local media. If they can't make it, be sure to take photos yourself (Cub Scout and resident dancing, children serving cookies) and deliver it to the paper. Just be sure that you have worked with the executive director throughout this project. You don't want a photographer showing up and the executive director having no knowledge of it ahead of time.

A project like this will have accomplished several things, including the following:

- moved old inventory out of your store

- given something to a local facility

- brightened the day of a group of local seniors

- helped a scout troop with a project

- perhaps helped another local business or two (the dance studio will be acknowledged as being part of the festivities)

- provided media coverage for yourself, the facility, and any other businesses that were involved.

The benefits you will have incurred include:

- great publicity

- goodwill in the community

- name recognition with local scouts, the facility's board of directors, and other local businesses

- tax benefits.

The next time someone affiliated with the organization has a need for electronic equipment you will be the first person he calls because he remembers your generous gift. A poll done by *Working Woman* magazine a few years ago showed that people prefer to deal with a company that supports a cause they believe in—provided that quality is equal—even if the price is a bit higher.

As business people, we don't always think about the fact that what we can no longer use is still useful to others. Remember that old saying, "One man's trash is another man's treasure"? Well, it can be especially true for excess inventory.

Take a look around at anything you may consider disposing of. Does anyone have a use for it? You might have an old desk or shelves that you are replacing. Can the local food bank use them? Maybe you have chipped dishes from your café that you don't want to serve customers anymore. Could a scout troop or after school program use them for a mosaic craft project? Perhaps you just changed from paper bags to a logo brand bag. I'll bet a daycare would be thrilled to have your leftovers. What do you do with flowers that are about to perish in your floral store? You might want to think about dropping them off at the hospital or nursing home and brightening the patients' days.

Before jumping into this, however, check with your attorney about liability. While you might think, "Wow! What a great idea!" the attorney might think, "Wow! What a risk!" For instance, we all look at our hungry population and think how terrible it is that leftover food from a restaurant isn't donated. What we don't think about is the potential for liability if donated food causes food poisoning in its recipients. So, talk to your attorney and evaluate any possible risk before donating anything. This way you can decide together what the risk is and what your comfort level is.

You should also seek professional advice from your accountant before assuming anything about the tax benefits you will receive. This would also be good advice to heed prior to selling anything to nonprofits without charging sales tax. All 501(c)(3)s are not exempt from paying state sales tax. This is an additional exemption that comes from individual states. Without the proper paperwork from the organization proving that they are exempt, you will be liable to pay the sales tax.

NON-TANGIBLE DONATIONS

Depending on the type of business you have, labor may make up the largest part of the charge to the customer. Obviously, the "product" attorneys, accountants, or consultants provide is ninety percent to 100 percent service. Other businesses, such as auto repair, beauty shops, and spas, will have a tangible product that they retail, but they will also factor in a substantial amount for labor or service.

A great way to give to a cause when budgets are extra tight is to charge for materials only. When negotiating with an organization, you can simply explain your desire to help to the best of your ability. Let them know exactly what that ability is and how it will benefit both of you.

As a businessperson, you might want to offer a discount even before you are asked. Here's what happened with an organization I know of.

Peggy Dolan, who founded and runs the Kelly Anne Dolan Memorial Fund in memory of her daughter, was looking for a banquet hall or hotel to hold a gala celebrating the organization's 25th year. There would be a cocktail reception, silent auction, dinner, and dancing to live music. The gala would serve as both a fundraiser and celebration of all the children helped in her daughter's name. It was to be held on a Friday or Saturday night in Philadelphia and would be a black tie affair. Tickets would be in the neighborhood of $100 per person.

As Peggy began her search for a place to hold this wonderful occasion, she discovered that suitable locations were quite expensive and difficult to find. Finally, she found a beautiful banquet hall with Old World charm. She loved the spot but discovered the price was probably not affordable.

The owner of the facility began talking to Peggy, who explained that her 6-year-old child had died after a long and rare illness. Peggy went on to explain that she and her late husband began this foundation to pay for uninsured costs of care related to a child's illness. They sometimes even paid for a child's funeral because the family couldn't afford it. This gala, she said, was to celebrate the fund's twenty-five years of service.

Since the hall was out of her budget, Peggy planned on leaving. Before she could, the owner made her an offer; if she would be willing to hold the event on Sunday rather than Friday or Saturday, he would give it to her at a huge discount.

As a result of the owner's offer, a fantastic gala was held on a Sunday night at Ballroom at the Ben, the former Ben Franklin Hotel in Philadelphia. Peggy couldn't stop gushing to everyone about how wonderful the owner was. His business was in the newspaper, and all of the people there—many of them executives from major corporations that frequently host events—would remember him the next time they needed a banquet hall.

In the above example, was this a kind gesture from the owner of the ballroom? Absolutely. Was it also a wise business move? You bet. Had he not offered the discount, the function might have been held elsewhere, and no one would have been aware of his business. The fact that he offered the discount rather than being asked for one made his gift all the more valuable and caused Peggy to talk about it more frequently.

Did he make any money? Perhaps. I certainly don't know his profit margin, but as long as his actual costs were covered, he lost nothing. Obviously, had the room been taken at the full price he would have brought in more money, but what if the room wasn't rented at all? He would have had no customers, no free advertising, and no goodwill within a new community. By offering this discount, he was able to gain all of the above with no outlay of capital.

In the area of goodwill, think about what we each share with our friends, families, and even strangers about service that we have or haven't received. The previous story was told to me by Peggy Dolan who was very touched by this businessman's generosity. Now, almost a year later I am telling everyone who reads this book. The point is that you never know where a good marketing strategy wrapped in kindness may go. This good deed occurred in Philadelphia and the story has now spread across the country.

Dave Hamby, former owner of Premier Auto Body in Texas, provides a great example of using this approach. Dave tried all kinds of advertising, even paying a huge amount of money for radio advertising spots. After about 100 radio spots aired and Dave received only one call, he decided to take a different approach. Having always been involved in his community, Dave began to really focus on his immediate surroundings for marketing ideas.

When the local Drug Abuse Resistance Education (DARE) program needed to have their car fixed, Dave volunteered to do it contributing the labor free of charge. The program only had to pay for the paint. In this case, Dave gave them more than just a hefty discount; he saved them a substantial amount of money that they could then put into programs to help the community.

So, did it benefit Dave? Because he had a tracking system— something that all large businesses have and many small businesses forget about —he was able to clearly see what worked and what didn't. We know that the radio spots didn't work for him. However, the DARE car was a whopping success. There were thirty cars in his shop during the following month—eleven of them could be directly attributed to the DARE car. That's more than one third!

Because the community support worked so well, Dave began sponsoring the local little league and soccer league. His company name was on the shirts as well as a billboard on the field. Everyone that saw one of the uniformed children was also seeing the name of Premier Auto Body. They may have had no need for an auto body shop at that particular moment, but odds are that when they did, Premier would leap into their minds.

Smart consumers will probably go to Premier and another shop for bodywork estimates. They might find that both have good records with the Better Business Bureau, but the other shop has a slightly lower price. What will their decisions be? Which shop will they go with?

They have seen Premier Auto Body as a sponsor on several kids' ball team shirts, they know about the DARE vehicle, and they even read in the paper that Dave serves on various charitable boards. The other shop, while slightly lower in price, has not sponsored any teams, and the owner says he just doesn't have time to work with charities. He says he keeps his expenses low so he can pass on the savings to his customers. That sounds good, but....

As they mull this over, there are a couple of things to consider. Ball teams exist mostly thanks to the generosity of businesses willing to pay for sponsorships. The same is true for charities. Most nonprofit boards consist of a diverse group of business leaders who believe in the cause. The Rotarians, Lions, Kiwanians, and other groups that participate in community projects are comprised of mainly business people. Because we as people believe that our communities need to be supported in order to survive, logic would tell us to support those businesses that support the community.

SERVICE IN YOUR COMMUNITY

While working and initiating a cause-related marketing campaign in your community is great, serving your community is wise marketing as well. What do I mean by serving your community?

Joining a service group such as Rotary, Lions, Soroptomist, Kiwanis, or Seratona is one great way. Members of these organizations are business people within your community who want to make a difference. You may find your next perfect cause-related marketing campaign within these groups.

To avoid joining the group and then realizing you don't like it, try to find out what their mission is and maybe even attend a meeting or two as a guest. For some groups such as Rotary you will have to be sponsored by a member and voted on prior to joining. Most of these organizations do wonderful work within their community and some even internationally.

Another way to serve your community is to serve on a committee or even on the board of an organization you've already been working with. Board members serve for various time frames—some may have a one-year appointment, while others have two- or three-year appointments. Frequently, organizations try desperately to find good people who will serve the organization and its mission well.

How is this marketing? In several ways. If you are appointed to the board, be sure that a press release and photo go to the paper. If there are appropriate trade magazines, send the same to them. Put it into your business newsletter, bulletin board, and Web site so that everyone knows. After all, this might be an organization that helped their family in the past.

I served on several local boards and committees and was a member and officer of Rotary while I had my retail business. I also got involved with the Phoenixville

Violence Prevention Committee because it is a cause to which I have a strong personal commitment. I worked with the children at a local school to make a peace quilt, a living quilt that traveled around the community. When the quilt was done, I called the newspaper, and they sent a photographer.

The photo showed me holding this wonderful quilt made by the children. The cut line read, "Phoenixville Violence Prevention Committee and the children of Barkley Elementary School along with the YMCA make a quilt depicting peace. The quilt can be seen at the celebration in Reeves Park on Sunday. After that, it will appear throughout town. Peggy Linial, owner of Ceramics by ME, Inc., has coordinated the efforts."

So, while I was personally working on a committee that I believe in and, frankly, feel should be in every community, I was still referred to in the media as a local business owner. My business did pick up the cost of the fabric, which was nominal, and one of my staff members cut all of the squares. So we really did work on the project as a business, but I never approached the paper with the notion that my business was even a part of the story. Yet, there it was—front page—my business involved in the community again.

While serving on boards, you will learn of ideas that you may want to be involved in from a business standpoint. For instance, if you owned a local paint store, you may decide that you would like to be involved in a project fixing up the homes of seniors in your area. Perhaps you are an artist or graphic designer. You may be the perfect person to work on a project beautifying your downtown area or designing a mural for a historic building, library, or school.

You may also run across functions that you feel are in conflict with your business. If this is the case, feel free to excuse yourself from participation. Let's say you own a daycare facility that caters to primarily fundamentalist Christians. It would be ludicrous and probably a quick way to commit professional suicide for you to participate in a pro-choice event. If you own and operate a health food store that caters to vegans, you probably would choose not to participate directly in an event such as a pig roast.

Serving on a board also allows you to come up with some very creative ideas for fundraising that can benefit both your business and the organization you serve. I was fortunate to serve on the board of St. Peter's Place, an independent housing facility for seniors. Dena Newkirk, the facility's director, tried to be sure that there were activities and teas and lots of other fun things for the residents to do. She was always ready for a new idea. (When you find someone with such open-mindedness, cherish it, because it's rare!)

After a pre-holiday board meeting, I mentioned to Dena that I had a ton of ceramic Christmas ornaments. I suggested that we have the scouts paint them and bring them over to St. Peter's Place. The residents could hang them with the scouts, and then they could have punch and cookies. Dena thought it was a great idea but wanted to know what it would cost since she had a limited budget. I told her if she would call and make arrangements for the paper to be there, get a good picture, and mention that we donated the ornaments, I would cover the cost.

Dena was thrilled—she had a Christmas event at no cost. The residents were thrilled too—they had a party, and it was with children, which they enjoy tremendously. The scout leader was thrilled because her troop got to paint ornaments without cost and they got a community service project completed. The kids were thrilled—they got to paint and have a party, and they loved being with the older people who shared past Christmas stories with them. Finally, the paper was thrilled—they got a great photo of a child and a senior resident hanging ornaments together. I was beyond ecstatic—what more could I have possibly wanted!

STAFF SERVICE

Another area that promotes a cause-related marketing program is staff support and service. A few years ago, I worked for a publishing company that published textbooks for EMTs and paramedics. I was assigned an article on an air ambulance service in San Antonio, Texas. I was subsequently cleared to fly with the crew of the air ambulance for a day.

During the late afternoon, Scotty and Sondie, the crew I was with, asked if I'd like to go to a BBQ. "Uh, aren't we on duty?" was my response. Sondie explained that we'd be on back up call to another unit for a short period of time. Since part of their mission was education and community service, we were going to take the helicopter to a rural area where a fire department was having an annual BBQ. Sondie and Scotty would give a brief talk about the helicopter and then let the kids go on board to see the equipment.

Later when I spoke to Sondie, who along with being the flight nurse is also director of marketing for the service, she explained that they feel so strongly about educating the public about what they do that they created a policy within their department. Everyone is paid for forty hours; however, everyone works in the field only thirty-two hours. The remaining eight hours is spent educating the public. It may involve taking the helicopter out to a BBQ like we did or talking to a daycare program or a church group.

This has worked as a great CRM program. The service maintains contracts and is extremely well thought of among members of their field and the public. Beyond that, the staff is happy and attrition is low.

Several years ago, a restaurant in Chicago called Not Just Pasta became very involved in an organization that ran a restaurant for the homeless. Rather than step up in line and get food dumped on their paper plates, this restaurant gave homeless customers a menu, service, and meals served on china. Ed and his staff rotated shifts working there. They all believed in it and were happy to do it. Ed also sold artwork in his restaurant with a portion of the profits benefiting the restaurant for the homeless.

When I lived in Chicago, I ate breakfast at Not Just Pasta almost every Saturday morning. After eating there week after week, I finally read an article in the *Chicago Sun* about this restaurant for the homeless. It explained the philosophy of the organization and named several (all small independently owned) restaurants that were involved. You guessed it—Not Just Pasta was mentioned as one of the originators.

I later spoke with Ed and found that he believed that even though people were going through something horrible, their dignity should be protected. Since he was in the restaurant business, it was the only way he knew to help. He also said he would never have been able to have the restaurant without the help of others, so he was giving back the best way he could.

Since Not Just Pasta was a pretty small café, I had previously gone there only for breakfast. After hearing about what Ed did, I began eating there frequently for dinner. I also had the restaurant cater a business party as well as a holiday party at my home. I didn't compare prices; I didn't haggle. I simply hired him and felt as though I was helping in a small way. While I never discussed the good deeds done by Not Just Pasta with other patrons, I'm sure they were well aware of them. There was a fair amount of press concerning the restaurant's involvement, and hanging in the café itself was art that was sold to raise money for various charities. Frequently, a homeless person would come in and ask for coffee on a cold morning. I never saw anyone turned away; in fact they were often handed a hot loaf of bread or a sandwich. While it sounds a bit corny, there was always a sense of community and kindness in Not Just Pasta, and it was always filled with regular customers—an unusual occurrence in large urban areas.

While donating money or services is always a great idea and greatly appreciated by the recipient, sometimes giving of yourself is more gratifying. Giving as a company can also provide lasting business relationships. Your company will be viewed as a dedicated and committed group of people. As long as the cause is one that the entire staff feels is worthwhile, you have the added benefit of doing good while having some fun outside of day-to-day business operations.

When my father was in an extended-care rehabilitation unit at the local hospital he had to use a walker. Even though he was in his mid-eighties, he felt he was way too young to be using a walker. Dad had been a musician in his younger days playing with Tommy and Jimmy Dorsey, and music had always been his first love. I decided to take his walker one day and paint a variety of musical notes all over it. It was pretty wild! Many people in the hospital stopped to ask about it, which thrilled my father, who loved to be the center of attention.

One of the nurses told me that the other patients loved it and asked if I would paint some more walkers for the unit. Since I had the ceramics studio, I certainly had paint. I took three or four walkers at a time to the studio and the entire staff began painting. Some had flowers, others stars and moons, and some even a leopard print! We did the painting during the slower times at the studio, but of course customers were in and out and saw the walkers. When they asked what we were doing, we explained that it was a community service project for the hospital.

The development director at the hospital took pictures that were included in a newsletter. Out of the blue a month or so later, I got a phone call from the producer at WPVI, the ABC television affiliate in Philadelphia. He wanted to interview us and tape us painting the walkers at the hospital for a weekend news show. I mentioned the studio, and he agreed to come and shoot there first.

The TV station was working on a tight deadline and, of course, I needed the hospital's permission for the taping. The public relations director was away, but because of my involvement with Rotary I knew the hospital CEO and felt comfortable contacting him directly. While it was a great opportunity to have my business on a popu-lar TV show, it was an equally good opportunity for the hospital. The CEO agreed and taping was scheduled.

The segment aired about a month after it was taped. Our studio was shown with the pottery and jewelry-making even though the main theme was the painted walkers. The story mentioned that we provided this project as a service project at no cost to the hospital. We later received calls from areas that never would have heard of us had it not been for this newscast.

COLD, HARD CASH

If you feel at certain times that a cash donation is the most appropriate, you should know that monetary donations are always greatly needed and appreciated by charitable organizations. To get the biggest bang for your buck, so to speak, try to present your contribution in a more creative way than just writing a check and handing it over.

Perhaps you're a florist and you've decided that ten percent of your rose profits on Valentine's Day will be donated to the local nonprofit daycare center for their nature program. After getting the go ahead from the daycare center, contact the editor of your local paper. Explain about the center's nature program—that the children are taught the importance of nature and how to grow their own flowers and vegetables. Explain the donation that you intend to make and that you will actually help the children plant the garden. Ask if they would send a photographer to get a shot of the children breaking ground (make sure this is planned before Valentine's Day) and run the story. If for some reason they aren't staffed to do it, ask if you can provide the photo and story.

A photo of the florist handing a check to the organization's director will not have nearly the same impact as a photo of him helping the children actually plant a rose bush. It also won't be as appealing for the paper to print.

The headline might read something like; "Local florist John Doe of ABC Flowers spent the morning digging and planting a rose bush at Happy Day Care with about seven young children. Doe expressed how important it is for youngsters to get to know about the care of plants when they are young. Appreciation of nature has been a mission for Doe, and this is his third year funding this program. For additional information, he can be reached at 221-2321."

In this case, you've given the money, which you felt was important, but you have also gotten some great publicity. The publicity certainly will help your business, and it might also encourage other individuals or businesses to contribute as well. You have actually helped your cause in three ways: 1) you donated money; 2) you actually involved the children; and 3) you brought much needed publicity to the organization.

It's important to remember that no matter what the size of your budget there are many creative ways to give. It's equally important to remember to promote what you do. While you are helping your business, you are also helping the organization. If you don't take advantage and promote your business at every opportunity, you will be unable to continue to make charitable gifts.

BUSINESS PROFILE

DAVE HAMBY INSURANCE AGENCY
206 West Main Street, Suite 104 • Round Rock, TX 78664
512-255-7000 • dhamby@austin.rr.com
Owner: Dave Hamby • Business: Insurance Agent

Due to the laws against "rebating" or promising donations on policies sold, insurance is a business that
requires some creativity in utilizing a cause-related marketing campaign. Dave has found a way. Texas is known
for their love of sports, and Dave takes advantage of this
by sponsoring baseball, soccer, and other teams in the
area. Yes, this is a wonderful way to support your community. But it also guarantees that the name of Dave's
company will be splashed on the chest of every child on
the teams. Every adult who attends the games will see
his company prominently displayed. It's also likely that
the teams will have their photos in the paper.

Dave also shows his support by joining civic organizations, working on various committees, such as Relay for
Life, and serving on local boards, such as a local charity
called For the Love of Christy.

I met Dave in Rotary where we're both active and was
amazed at how he ties his business to service in his community. To this day it has served him well.

CHARITY PROFILE

GREAT PLAINS ASSISTANCE DOGS FOUNDATION
PO BOX 513 • 920 Short Street • Jud, ND 58454
877-737-8364 • www.greatplainsdogs.com
gpadf@daktel.com • Contact: Mike Goehring

MISSION: To assist physically challenged individuals in gaining greater independence and autonomy by the use of a trained and certified assistance dog, and to do so without adding excessive financial burden to those using the program.

Great Plains Assistance Dogs placed their first dog in 1990. The organization began because a need existed—there was no other service locally. However, they do place dogs throughout the country.

The majority of inquiries for dogs come from those needing seizure dogs. Great Plains is known for their work and is considered a leader in placing dogs with those suffering from a seizure disorder. They are also one of few that train dual purpose dogs. This allows those that have multiple disabilities to have a service dog.

While it takes about $20,000 to train each dog, they offer a sliding scale for those who can't afford the full cost. Their belief is that if an individual contributes to the cost they will be more committed to maintaining a sense of independence as well. Based on need, some have paid as little as $100 down and $10 a month for the working life of the dog.

Dogs that, after training, are determined to be unable to work as service dogs are sold to good homes.

CHAPTER 6

Getting Publicity

The time has arrived. You have worked tirelessly to find an appropriate nonprofit to work with. You are comfortable with the partnership you have. You have a wonderful idea for a cause-related marketing campaign. Now, how do you attract publicity?

PAID ADVERTISING

First, I feel compelled to talk about paid advertising. It can be very expensive and, frequently, you will find through good tracking methods that it doesn't work well if you just do it sporadically. For ads to generate a profit, they need to run on a routine basis, which can be a costly venture.

You will be contacted by more places than you can imagine. There are regional specialty magazines, national magazines, radio and television stations, and even church bulletins that carry advertising, not to mention your local newspaper, neighborhood newsletters, chamber of commerce directories, and school publications.

In our case, children's birthday parties were a large part of business. For that reason we did spend a considerable amount of money on an ad in a regional family magazine that had a page for children's parties. By tracking each party scheduled, we found that these ads were worth the expenditure.

We also ran ads in a few church bulletins. These ads, ultimately weren't worth much in return, so we discontinued them after six months, but I know of a couple of contracting businesses that felt it was their best-spent money.

Whenever a story ran about us in our local paper, we were inundated with calls and customers. Unfortunately, when we ran a regular business ad in the same paper, we got very little response. However, a community paper has to have ads to survive, and they had supported us extremely well, providing us with more editorial space than we could have ever afforded to purchase. For those reasons, we regularly advertised in the special sections— children's coloring pages, bridal sections, and other sections that were applicable to our business. We also made sure those ads were large sizes in order to get the greatest amount of exposure. We found that those ads did generate business for us; but had they not, we would have still run them as a sign of our support. Frankly, supporting your local paper is just good business. As both businesses and community members, we should be saddened if our local newspapers fold.

NEWSPAPERS

Newspapers are probably the most easily accessible media available to small businesses. Choose the paper you want to approach by considering where you are located, the type of business you operate, and customers you plan to attract.

For instance, if you own a bed and breakfast then you will welcome publicity in distant areas. This can let people know why they should stay with you when they come to your city. You'll also want local publicity, so that families in town will know of a great place to recommend to their out-of-town guests.

On the other hand, if you are a sign maker in Boise, Idaho, working fervently to get press, you might not find it beneficial to spend a lot of time trying to get a story in the *Boston Globe*. Concentrating on your local and neighboring papers may be a more cost effective way to utilize your time.

Getting the Press

Many years ago, working at Moore Regional Hospital, in Pinehurst, North Carolina, I learned the value and impact of a story in the newspaper. On occasion, I would be contacted by a reporter whom I thought had magically found out about an event we had. I discovered later that Derry Walker, our public relations person, had been sure that the paper was well aware of what was going on at the hospital. Derry was armed with his camera at nearly every event the hospital had. Occasionally, the newspaper would send a reporter and a photographer as well. Usually, within a day or so of the event there would be an article—anywhere from a blurb to a full story—in one or both of our local papers.

The result was exactly what we wanted—the community residents knew what was going on at our hospital, we were seen in a positive light, and, because we were in the media so frequently, it was assumed that we were always doing good. Moore Regional had and still has a good reputation within their community (i.e., their customer base).

While a public relations force is commonplace in large businesses or corporations, it rarely exists in small businesses, especially start-ups. Small business owners have to competently handle public relations in addition to handling every other aspect of the business.

When I started my business, I read many articles and books and attended seminars that described appropriate press releases. Most talked about format: one inch margin on the left, two inches down from the top, three inches from the bottom. You get the idea. It can be a bit intimidating for the novice, but is it really necessary? Will the wrong format cause your press release to be sent to the round file under an editor's desk?

I decided the easiest way to know for sure was to ask the editors. So, not being overly shy, I sauntered down to the paper and asked to speak to the editor or an assistant if he was busy. The editor at the time was happy to meet the owner of a new business in town. We chatted for a moment, during which time he suggested they do a story about my new business. Wow, I could live with that!

He told me that a specific format didn't matter to him as long as the following questions were answered: WHO,

WHAT, WHERE, and WHEN. For this book, I spoke with several editors, all of whom have echoed the same sentiments.

About six months later, the same editor decided to hold a seminar on writing press releases. I, along with about ten other community members, attended. I was the only business owner there—most were people working with very small nonprofits. Most had also sent press releases to the paper that had not been printed, and they wanted to know why.

The editor showed a variety of rejected press releases (with identifying data omitted of course). A few of the mistakes may shock you. Several began with such demands as, "I advertise in your paper and want this printed," or "You must print this or I will cancel my subscription." Still others gave incomplete information, no contact information, or were scribbled illegibly on notepaper.

Know Your Paper

Obviously, a large daily paper like the *Washington Post* and *Los Angeles Times* are going to have different criteria for what goes in their paper than the *Greenville Gazette*.

Since time is always a huge concern to the small business owner, you'll need to make a few decisions. How much time do you want to devote to attempting to get into the large daily paper rather than your smaller community paper? Which will have the most impact on your revenue?

Before you make this decision, ask yourself a couple of questions: 1) Which paper would most likely be read by potential customers? 2) How much space would I get in the paper? 3) Where will my coverage be in the paper?

A paper that covers an area like Los Angeles needs to write for its audience. If you have a small bakery, is it likely that someone living fifty miles south of L.A. will come to your shop thirty miles north of the city for your event?

In such a case, your efforts may be better spent approaching the local community paper where ninety percent of the readers are close by. Both you and your charity may discover a much better financial gain with this method.

How much space and where that space will be are important factors in determining the paper you want to approach. Is a two-sentence insert on the community calendar of the huge daily going to be as effective as a picture and story on the cover of the smaller local paper? Most readers' busy schedules will draw them to a picture to see what the story is about before reading the full text. The likelihood of a couple of sentences being read in the calendar or towards the back of a paper is pretty slim.

Large Metropolitan Papers

Margaret Holt, an editor at *The Chicago Tribune*, says one of the most important tasks a business owner can complete is to read and be familiar with the paper before you approach them. For a paper such as the *Tribune*, there are many sections, each having its own editor. It certainly behooves you to know what section is most appropriate for your story and to then approach that editor.

If your event or story could be covered by one of several sections, send a copy of your release to all of the appropriate editors. At a large paper, if it isn't appropriate for their particular section, an editor may not forward it to the editor of another section. After all, they are extremely busy and have numerous daily requests on their desks. Certainly, it is always a courtesy to mention that you have also submitted the information to Ms. Jones in the sports department or Mr. Smith in the suburban news department.

A suggestion from another editor [who wished to remain nameless] at a large urban paper was to try to get the paper to partner with you for an event. If it is a small, community event, they may still be quite open to show their support by being a joint sponsor. It provides goodwill in the community, which can equate to additional subscribers and advertisers for the paper. The added benefit, according to this editor, is that most large papers will shamelessly cover their own events and will do so in several different sections.

With larger papers, you may need to be a bit creative in garnering editorial space. As Holt says, "It's not our job to see that you get your fair share." After all, there are many people looking for the same coverage. How can you be creative in getting the attention? You will need to find the news hook.

Make publicity a part of your business plan. Just as you begin thinking about your holiday merchandise, special sales, and other promotions early in the year, plan your publicity the same way. If you own a small independent bookstore, read the book reviews in your paper and know who writes them. If there is a columnist for the book section, read his or her articles regularly, and if you enjoy a particular column, send a note to the columnist saying as much.

Read the business section and get to know which reporters and columnists cover what types of stories. Again, drop them a line if you particularly like or agree with something they write. Holt reminds us that we are all people and like to have our work recognized and appreciated. The added benefit, she says, is that down the road, when you send a letter about an event going on to support a charity, columnists may remember your other kind words and give you a plug in their columns. This could be above and beyond any additional coverage you've received.

Local, Community Papers

If your business is in a smaller town, this is probably where you want to concentrate your efforts. Most communities will have a local daily or weekly paper that really caters to that particular community. According to Andy Marks, editor of the *Round Rock Leader*, an award-winning community paper in Texas, these papers are an integral part of the community. Marks suggests that you "approach the paper like a friend." Community papers are typically very approachable and operate in a "hand-shake" atmosphere. The editors don't typically have secretaries screening their calls or publicists handling media requests. By and large, they are very happily a well-known part of the community. "I much prefer a face to face visit with a community member as opposed to being contacted by a company's publicist," says Marks.

You will have a little more flexibility in working with a local paper, in part because of their size and in part because they are usually a bit more ingrained in your particular community. The editor of the local will probably be a bit more accessible, but remember that they are also stretched for time and staff.

Stan Huskey, editor of *The Times Herald*, a daily in Pennsylvania, suggests paying particular attention to the news end of the story. New products or the arrival of holiday merchandise would not be news, but if one of your new holiday lines has been handmade by children at a local shelter with the profits going back to that organization, that is newsworthy, and your chances of having the story covered are good. Make sure to mention the newsworthy aspect up front. Remember that editors get many press releases daily and have a minimum amount of time to look at them. Huskey always asks himself if the readers will care about the story, and he looks for stories that will impact the largest number of readers.

Like most other editors, Huskey also emphasizes being sure to always include WHO, WHAT, WHERE, and WHEN in any press release. If all of this information is not included, there is a good chance that your request for coverage will not be honored.

Many small local papers will allow you to submit your own photograph to be published. Frequently, in a small venue there are minimal budgets and staff to provide a photographer for every event. (In contrast, most large metropolitan papers have sufficient staff coverage twenty-four hours a day and would normally not consider using your photographs.)

Most papers prefer action photos, since people doing something is far more interesting than people just standing in a line. It's important to identify everyone in the photo. If the staff is on a tight deadline and does not have time to contact you, photos with unidentified people could be excluded altogether.

E-mail, fax, or send a press release about your event as soon as you know about it. You should follow up with a phone call as the event gets closer. One of the mistakes occasionally made with community papers is that they are contacted too close to the event to cover it. You can't expect to call today and have coverage tomorrow. The paper would love to provide the news to the community, and certainly you and your charity would benefit greatly from the publicity. However, if the paper is not contacted far enough in advance, everyone misses out on the opportunity.

Most of the editors that I spoke to at community papers welcomed the opportunity to get to know the members of the business community. When you start your business, go in and introduce yourself. As a courtesy, call first and ask for a convenient time to stop by. After all, papers have deadlines they need to meet, and the last thing you want is for either of you to leave with a bad first impression because of poor timing.

When you meet, let the editor know who you are and why your business exists. Share your feelings about cause-related marketing. They might even know of a worthwhile charity that could benefit greatly from your efforts. Your local paper is the pulse of the community and a great resource that shouldn't be ignored.

Newspaper Tips

I asked all of the editors that I spoke with for tips on what to do and not do. They all echoed the same suggestions:

- You are not entitled to automatic editorial coverage just because you advertise in the paper. News and advertising are two entirely separate entities. In fact, the editors of the large metropolitan papers say that a section editor may not even be aware of whether you advertise or not.

- Be polite. While this just sounds like common sense, most of the editors had a story to share about someone demanding to have an item run for a variety of reasons—from being friends with the publisher's uncle's mother-in-law to being a subscriber or an advertiser. Remember what your mother taught you—"please" and "thank you" go a very long way.

- Don't think that because you send a request that it will automatically be honored. There may be many reasons why it simply can't be published at this time. The event may have already had a tremendous amount of publicity, your request may not seem newsworthy, or there may simply not be room or time right now. Don't let this prevent you from sending a press release or calling the editor for the next event.

- Be prepared. If the paper has sent a photographer, chances are that he or she is heading from your photo shoot directly to another, so be ready when they get there.

- Give the paper plenty of lead time. If you want coverage, especially if a photographer is involved, contact the paper at least a week in advance. Feel free to follow up closer to the event, however.

RADIO

Radio stations frequently cover wide geographic areas, and again, as with newspapers and television, you are going to be fighting for time with many other equally worthy organizations and businesses. However, think of the amount of time we spend in our cars listening to and bonding with some of those on-air personalities, not to mention the radio playing at doctors' and dentists' offices and many other businesses day in and day out. The fight for coverage might be well worth it.

The larger the station and market, the more layers of administration there will be. For instance, I spoke with

Rich Rushforth, the station manager at 102.5 in Southern Pines, North Carolina. He said that these days the phrase "do more with less" is a common theme in community stations.

With that in mind, don't just saunter by the radio station one day and ask them to put together a free announcement for you. He suggests you call and make an appointment. You may want to speak with the public service director who can let you know if your event would fall under that category. Remember that there are strict guidelines for Public Service Announcements (PSAs), and be sure to follow whatever instructions are given by the public service director.

Be sure that all information is included when you provide the information to the public service director. You will want to treat this like a press release for a newspaper. They will need to know WHO, WHAT, WHERE, and WHEN. Current contact information is also critical.

In a larger market, you may need to start by contacting the marketing department. Discuss with them exactly what it is that you are doing and what you want from them. After evaluating your proposal, the marketing department may decide that the airtime you are requesting doesn't qualify as a PSA and would need to be purchased.

With a larger market, your best opportunity may be to have the charity that you are partnering with make the initial contact. Because many businesses have public relations firms or publicists spending entire days attempting to spin a story for coverage, the marketing or program departments are rightfully a bit skeptical.

In the smaller community, it is likely that the contact you speak with at the radio station may even be familiar with your business or the charity. Who knows, he or she may be a current or future customer. Much like the community newspaper, a local radio station's personalities or program manager may actually live right there. They will most likely gravitate towards local community service since that is their audience base.

Another opportunity with a radio station is the on-air interview. For this, you will go to the station for a brief interview with the host. Occasionally, this interview may take place over the phone. I frequently did this when I ran a support group for heart patients at Moore Regional Hospital. It was usually bright and early in the morning, and I had the opportunity to let people know what meeting we had coming up and talk very briefly about the featured speaker.

At that point, I was on the nonprofit side, but I always mentioned the guest speaker at the conference who might be a physician, nutritionist, physical therapist, or even pharmaceutical company coming to speak about a new cardiac drug. These radio mentions benefited their practices as well.

These interviews are usually light, fun, and pretty informal. You should be prepared with the message you want to convey, succinctly and quickly. Be sure to make the nonprofit benefiting from your service or event the main focus of your message. You don't want to leave the listener with the feeling that you are using an organization solely to get ahead. Remember, too, that on the radio no one can see your expressions or any body language. You have only your voice to get your message across. Practice ahead of time what you have to say until you are happy with the way that it sounds.

Often, when you're interviewed you will be asked to provide questions you want to answer on the air. This makes the interviewer's job and your own easier. You can be reasonably sure that information you want the public to hear will be presented. Again, be sure not to sound self-serving.

If you are geographically close to the station, let them know that you are always happy to fill in should a guest suddenly cancel. Many stations will be thrilled to know that there is someone who "knows the ropes" and is ready to step in at any time. This gives you the opportunity to build a relationship with key media in town while getting publicity for your business and your charity. The station will be very appreciative of your help since they won't have to scatter for filler in an emergency. This turns into a win–win–win situation, which is always great.

Steve Allan, program manager of WASH and WBIG in Washington, D.C., says it is not impossible to have an on-air personality attend your function. He suggests that you contact the personality directly and be honest about exactly what you want from them. (Are they there to drive **attendance**? Do you need an emcee?) Some other stations suggest that you check with the individual station since some on-air personalities work solely through an agent.

What about a remote broadcast? This is also a possibility depending on the situation. It is more likely in a regional situation than a huge urban market. Rushforth reminds us that we need to find a reason for it to benefit the radio station, whether it's increasing the number of listeners, improving public image, or boosting revenue dollars.

Several stations also suggest that you inquire whether your charitable partner is able to invite a media professional to sit on its board of directors. Not only will they then have a personal interest in the works of the charity, but also the charity will have a media savvy person to advise them.

Radio Tips

- Contact them in writing far in advance. Follow up with a phone call after they have had a chance to review your request.

- Don't forget the basics—WHO, WHAT, WHERE, and WHEN—along with contact names and numbers.

- Be prepared. Know what you are going to say and do it in a concise manner.

- Since you want something for free, be persistent yet polite. It is up to you to find an angle that convinces

the station that their listeners are going to be interested in what you are promoting.

TELEVISION

When looking to expand your customer base beyond
your local boundaries, the greatest exposure you can
have is television. At Ceramics by ME, we managed to be
in feature segments of the local ABC, CBS, NBC, and
FOX affiliates as well as on local cable. We were also featured several times on the Discovery Channel's *Home
Matters* and The Learning Channel's *Wedding Story*.

The most exposure we got was on the FOX show *Good
Day Philadelphia*. This show was the typical morning
show, consisting of variety and news. I knew that *Good
Day Philadelphia* had a reporter named Grover who once
or twice a week filmed a short segment at an area business performing some activity—maybe cooking or
making a craft. So I sent the producer a press package
that included the material (which was brand new to the
industry) that we used to make silver jewelry. I also
included pieces of jewelry in each stage of the process so
that he could really see how easy it is to use. I mentioned
that we would love for Grover to come to our studio and
make some jewelry.

I followed up by phone a couple of weeks after I sent
everything. Since the show aired from 7 a.m. to 9 a.m., I
phoned the producer in the afternoon. The last thing I
wanted to do was try to reach him when it was clear he'd
be in a great rush. The producer spoke to me and said

they'd keep it in mind, but he didn't sound overly enthused. I thanked him and said I looked forward to speaking again.

About a month went by, and, not one to give up, I called again. I really wanted these two minutes of exposure. This time I had notes in front of me to make every pitch I could think of—the ease, the fun, the popularity. Everything he hears from everyone else!

During this pitch I casually mentioned that we were making logos of The Kelly Anne Dolan Memorial Fund and selling them with the bulk of the proceeds going to help this foundation. The producer said, "Now that's a story!" He wanted to know why I didn't mention it before. He'd call me back as soon as he could fit me in.

About a week later, he called on a Thursday and said they were going to send a crew and the weather person/anchor to us on Monday. From 6 a.m. to 9 a.m., every fifteen minutes, the show would cut to Sue for her weather report and would show her making a piece of jewelry. I would get to talk about The Kelly Anne Dolan Memorial Fund and the silver jewelry. Sue also gave a tour of the studio and talked about everything else we did as well. It was a great experience, and we had a few minutes of exposure eleven different times throughout the broadcast.

This is an example of the publicity a cause-related marketing campaign can get for you. If we had had Grover demonstrating our jewelry making, it would have been a very brief segment. Truthfully, as far away as our town was from Philadelphia, we may have never even gotten the coverage at all. However, by talking about what we were doing for someone else, we received extended coverage, as did our partnering charity.

This reiterates the importance of thinking about your story's angle before you contact the station. I was very lucky that the producer picked up the angle just from chatting, but that will rarely happen. Tony Bonilla, the assistant news director at KTVU in Oakland, California says, "It's up to you to tell me why I should care about a story." Of course, he's right. It's our job to sell the story.

If you are pitching to the news, you should contact the assignment desk. According to Pat Tanaka, assistant news director at KEYE in Austin, Texas, the assignment desk acts like a filter for the newsroom. They will keep a day file of news releases of what is happening that day.

Just as with all other media, you should know your show before you contact them. This means watching a few of the news broadcasts. Do they have a feature segment? Do they highlight businesses and charities? If so, is it on the 7 a.m., 5 p.m., or 11 p.m. news? Before you contact anyone you should be aware of exactly what they do and when.

Imagine how insulting it would be if someone came into your completely vegan café and asked for a T-bone steak and whether you give early bird specials. Not only are they asking for something you don't carry, but they want a discount! If you don't know your market, this is exactly what you will be doing.

If you discover that the station has a morning show or another show that you find more appealing for your market, contact the producer. Let them know why you chose their show and why their viewers will care about your endeavor. As in all other media, you will have to let the producer know why they should care and where the story is.

When contacting either the assignment desk or a producer, you will want to begin your press release with the news side. These people are fielding many, many different news pieces from the very serious to the human relation side. They need to be hooked by your release in an instant.

After you write it up, set it aside, look at it again later, and tweak it. Have someone you trust take a look and give you an honest opinion about its "grab appeal." Did they have questions right away? You may discover that it still needs a bit of revision.

Bonilla suggests that if you have had previous media coverage, mention it or send clips if it was in a newspaper. You've probably noticed, that once something appears in one medium you are likely to see it with a slightly different twist in others.

When we were interviewed by the local station about the walkers we painted for the local hospital, I mentioned that we had been on the *Home Matters* show on the Discovery Channel. The producer from the news show contacted the *Home Matters* producer and was able to get footage to weave into his segment about us.

One producer said the reality is it always helps to know someone. Not that it guarantees airtime, but it can help in getting your story idea seen by the appropriate person. So, if you know someone who has a contact don't hesitate to use it. Perhaps one of the charity's board members has worked with someone at the news before and can make an introduction.

Several of the news directors I spoke with prefer to be contacted by the charity. They are not necessarily averse to being contacted by the business, but that does send up a bit of a red flag. The bottom line, though, according to one director, is either the story or event is newsworthy or it's not. Newsworthiness for the news segments means that your event or cause will improve lives and/or benefit the community.

A warning that comes from Tanaka is that once you have contacted the news, be ready. They work with short notice. She also advises that you have your thoughts in order. You will have very little time to impress the viewer while still being genuine.

If you have any concerns about being on camera, have someone else speak for you. The last thing you want is to either freeze before the camera or continually repeat "uh" or "um." It may help to videotape a mock interview in preparation. This will give you an opportunity to see how you come across to the public. Many outplacement firms actually use this technique for job interviews. Rarely do we appear on camera the way we think we do.

Remember that your objective is to make a lasting impression on the public to promote both your business and your charity. You will have to do it, most likely, in 60 seconds or less. The other advantage to doing a mock interview is that you will be able to time yourself so that you are sure to get across the important aspects. Can you imagine how heartsick you would be if during your interview on the evening news you talk about your event, but are cut off before you give the address or name the benefiting charity?

For newscasts, the other occurrence you will have to be prepared for is the chance of breaking news. When this happens, all bets are off. The stations will be scrambling to keep up with the breaking story. Taped special segments can also be preempted.

This happened to us after September 11. We had been taped for a consumer segment on the 5 p.m. newscast. It was taped in July and was to air September 12. Well, everything was cancelled for round-the-clock coverage of the attack. Even after some parts of the country got back to more normal broadcasting, the coverage in Pennsylvania, only a couple hours away from New York, remained focused on the events. Our segment finally aired in January 2002.

If you are a small, community business working with a small community charity, how can an appearance on a national show help either of you? There are a couple of answers to that. First, brochures you produce will always benefit from the phrase "As seen on...." Second, the local newspapers will want to cover the fact that you are being featured on a national show. Just before we were on *Home Matters*, we contacted our large regional daily newspaper. We landed the full-page weekend cover of the business section with the heading, "Local Business to be Featured on the Discovery Channel This Week." We couldn't have asked for more than that.

TV Tips

- Make sure your story has news appeal. You must know and be able to tell the program director where the news in the story is and how it relates to the show's audience.

- Don't be too wordy in your first contact. Since program directors have precious little time, you need to capture their attention in a sentence or two. Remember that television works in very short segments, so your entire story may have to be told in just sixty seconds. (One minute actually lasts a lot longer than it would seem, so don't let that deter you.) The producer wants to be sure you are capable of this before scheduling you.

- Have your thoughts in order before you air. I can't stress the importance of this enough. In such a short time frame, you must have your thoughts organized into bulleted points, and they must be well-rehearsed so that nothing is left out. If you are taping a seg-ment, it's not as crucial, but frequently you will be live so there is no going back. I suggest you practice by taping yourself. If you are at all uncomfortable in front of the camera, have an employee or another representative get your message across.

- Let the news assignment desk or producer know why they should care. In the first few seconds of a phone conversation or a written pitch, you must get your message across. You want the person assigning stories to feel that this simply has to be on the air because the viewers will want to know what you are saying. Remember, you will be up against many others vying for that snippet of airtime.

- Know the show and its market. Be sure that you know the show before you pitch them. Imagine the impression you would leave if you pitched MTV for a function targeted to the senior audience. You would have wasted their time and yours. When you had an event that did match their audience, you would probably have a hard time getting through again.

- Be prepared for coverage as soon as you pitch something. Many shows, especially news shows, work in a very short time frame. If you contact them today, you need to be prepared if they say, "Be here tomorrow!"

MAGAZINES

You may think that the publicity from a national magazine will not provide much for your local business, but national publicity can easily generate local attention. Much in the way that we received great press in the local paper prior to appearing on television, the same can occur with magazine articles.

Contact the editor of your local paper letting them know what magazine you will be in, which issue, when it will hit the stands, and why you are featured in it. They may opt to do a story either before it comes out, or, more likely, right after it comes out, but while it is still on the news stands. If you are in a smaller community, there is a great chance that you will be featured on the front page with the charity's coordinator holding a copy of the magazine.

Be sure to contact not just your local paper but also any surrounding newspapers. If your business has done something worthwhile enough to enjoy national publicity, people will hop in the car and drive farther than they normally would to shop at your business.

You will also want to contact any local television or radio talk shows. There is a good chance that they will want to interview both you and the organization you are helping.

Before contacting a magazine, make sure its target audience will be interested in your story. Perhaps you are a haberdasher who donates hats to women undergoing chemotherapy. Most women's magazines would be appropriate to contact, while *Field and Stream*, although applauding your altruism, will probably not run the story.

According to Nancy Clark, deputy editor of *Family Circle* magazine, most stories are pitched to them by freelance writers via a written proposal. She also says that it is perfectly acceptable for the business owner to send a cover letter along with clips from local coverage.

While all editors have their own preferences for how to be contacted, Clark and several others suggest that a fax is the least effective. The reason for this varies, but the fact that they have to be sorted and sent to the appropriate person at the magazine is the main concern. For this reason, you may want to consider sending your information via standard mail or e-mail. It may be well worth the cost of a phone call to the magazine to ask how the editor prefers to receive queries. Since this is a huge part of their business, it is likely that the receptionist will know the answer.

Read the magazine's masthead to find the appropriate editor to submit your query to. Also, be sure to read the submission guidelines first. They can often be found on the Web site, or you can contact the magazine for them.

If you would like to actually submit the article, but don't feel you are the best to write it, your charitable partner may have a person on staff or on the board that is qualified to do it. If not, you can always look for a freelance writer. If there is a writer you know of who is trying to break into magazines, perhaps a reporter at your paper or a newsletter writer for a company, this may be a wonderful and much-appreciated opportunity for him or her. You will get your article submitted by a professional writer, which would be helping you and your charity, and the writer may have another published article to add to their portfolio.

Magazine Tips

- Before submitting a query for an article, check the masthead to find the correct editor. Because staff may have changed after the magazine went to press, it might be a good idea to call the office and double check the information. There is nothing worse than sending your query to an editor who is no longer on staff.

- Remember that a monthly magazine plans its stories several months in advance. For this reason, you want to be sure that any event you suggest a story about is not taking place for at least four to six months down the road. An even better idea would be to discuss an ongoing partnership so that the magazine has more options about timing.

- If you are submitting a story or idea, be sure to get a copy of their submission guidelines prior to sending it. You should also be aware that you will probably not get a response for several weeks. Their submission guidelines should spell all of this out for you. If you have not heard from them after a reasonable time, feel free to follow up with an e-mail or phone call.

- Most importantly, as with all media, know the magazine prior to submitting a query. Take the time to read a couple of copies. Not only will this keep you from wasting your time and the editor's, but you may know exactly what department or feature your event or partnership fits in, and you can tailor your pitch to it.

BUSINESS PROFILE

STELLULAR WEB PROGRAMMING
320 Ash Lane • White Haven, PA 18661
570-443-0628 • www.stellulardesign.com
Owner: Theresa Stachowiak
Business: Web site design and programming

A former medical technologist, Theresa chose to stay home and raise her children while volunteering in the community. She quickly discovered her love for computers and the Internet. As her children got older, Theresa combined her creativity and business skills to design Web sites. Soon after, Stellular Web Programming was born.

Always a supporter of children's charities, Theresa has worked with Make-A-Wish Foundation for many years. Currently, Theresa and Stellular Web Programming have gone into a local school to teach the children about computers. They will also be guiding the older children as they design a Web page.

Theresa believes her talents are a gift from God and that both she and her company have received far more than they have given.

Stellular Web Programming designed my Web site—www.marketingfromtheheart.com.

CHARITY PROFILE

HEARTS AND HOOVES
608 West 12th • Austin, TX 78701
512-585-5426 • www.heartsandhooves.org
quietswanmover@juno.com • Contact: Veronique Matthews

MISSION: To teach owners of miniature horses to housebreak, socialize, and train their animals to be used in pet therapy for institutional settings and homebound patients.

This is a new organization that has recently received its 501(c)(3) status as a nonprofit organization.

Veronique, who was a horse massage therapist for over six years, discovered she had breast cancer. After a double mastectomy and no insurance, she also discovered that pain now occurred when massaging large horses.

A neighbor then gave her a miniature horse, and she found a new happiness. She began taking it with her when she would visit friends, and discovered the joy that it brought to others and how it lifted their spirits.

Veronique then began training her miniature to visit disabled children in schools and nursing homes. She now owns six miniatures, one of whom can even climb into the bed with a patient for an extra snuggle.

Veronique and her horses visit many schools and homes at no cost to pick up the spirits of those who need it. Hearts and Hooves plans to expand to train horses and their owners around the country.

Both Veronique and her organization are a huge inspiration. Hearts and Hooves is a perfect example of a community organization that would be a wonderful match for a community business in a cause-related marketing endeavor.

CHAPTER 7

Everyone's Found Me— Now What?

Almost from the day you open your doors, you will begin to receive requests to donate to one organization or another. They may ask for a product for a silent auction, a cash donation for a charity, or they could be soliciting for an ad in their program or directory. You will also be added to nearly every local charity's capital campaign fund drive.

If you are like we were, you will donate to everyone who asks. You want to attract business and believe that every person making a donation request is a potential customer. You're new and want everyone to like you and say nice things about your business. If you turn them down, you start to have visions of the talk at the grocery store about how awful that new business in town is—they wouldn't even help out little Susie's preschool auction! (They'll conveniently forget to mention that little Susie is their grandchild and that her preschool is six hundred miles away!)

Finally, I realized that we were giving away a huge amount of product, and it was costing us a great deal.

Actually, my accountant is really the one who noticed how much we were giving away with no real discretion. He suggested we set up some system that offered us a cost effective way to choose which organizations we'd support.

We began to collect those requests, explaining to people that while we completely understood how important and valuable their charity was, we had a committee that would look at all requests and make the decision. Some people balked a bit, but I tried to explain that we just had so many requests that this was what we needed to do. The added benefit was that, while people were used to dealing primarily with just me in the store, they understood that I wasn't making the decision alone.

Those who didn't understand our reasoning were typically those same people who were running into all of the local businesses trying to collect for one thing or another and didn't want to make another trip back. While that is certainly understandable, we rarely made an exception to the committee rule.

Those exceptions that we did make were for a small item or gift certificate. They were requested by regular customers and generally were for a church, school, or scouting event. We made one other exception: a few events where children came in and asked for an item.

In our community, the middle school presented a show every year where the performing children solicited businesses to advertise in their program. I never turned them down. I admired their moxie, since I'm sure it wasn't easy to go door to door and ask businesses for this support.

For another regular event, third graders at a local elementary school had a math competition, the winners of which could choose a gift from a prize box. These kids very shyly stopped by every year, and we gave them several little items to include.

If you don't have a business that caters to children, you might want to consider purchasing and keeping in your drawer a few packets of McDonald's coupons or something similar for when children make requests.

MAKING THE EVALUATION

As the requests come pouring in, you will have to set up a system to make the decision as to whose requests you will honor and what types of donations you are able to provide. You may also want to keep a small reserve for those situations—like those mentioned above—when you just can't turn someone down.

You and your accountant will have to decide how much money and merchandise you want to donate within a certain time frame. Think through what you are able to give in a specific amount of time—say a year—before you write your policy in stone. Twenty-five dollars doesn't seem like such a large contribution, but imagine if you get just ten requests per month. That's $3,000 in one year. How will that work into your budget? Will it affect your support of your main partner charitable organization if you've chosen one?

Once you have this decided, you will need to come to an agreement about who will make the decisions. What is the benefit of forming a committee to mull over requests? When someone is asking for a donation, you don't want to have to rush to decide at that moment, so this gives you some time. Do you really want to be the person who takes full responsibility for turning down a cause that your customer feels passionately about? How would you feel if the situation were reversed and a business owner said, essentially, "No— your cause isn't my cause"?

In Chapter 3, I mentioned being turned down by Barnes and Noble for a donation to a silent auction I was organizing. I received a nice letter from the company explaining that they only support literacy causes, so they could not honor my request. If their community representative had just said "no" on the spot, I would likely not be shopping there for books in the future. Because they took my request into consideration and had a sound reason for turning it down, I respected their decision and did not change my opinion of the store.

Even if your committee is very informal, people in your community will perceive it as a more formal business strategy than many small businesses have. They will understand that you have to make decisions that are in the best interest of your business and will appreciate that you are carefully considering their request.

FORMING THE COMMITTEE

In our case, the committee consisted of my partner, my small staff, and myself. My business partner was an accountant, so he provided a valuable point of view in all discussions. My staff was a very close-knit group. It was also very diverse in that we had staff members in several different age groups—college students, young professionals who worked for us part-time, and moms with children in the local school system. Because of this diversity, I was able to run the requests by all staff members and get varied reactions. The other great advantage of including staff was that they had lived in the community longer than me and knew the worthiness of most of the organizations.

ORGANIZING THE INFORMATION

Ideally, you'll receive requests several months in advance, allowing you to put them in a tickle file. Sometimes you will have to make faster decisions about requests that come in at the last minute—perhaps within a matter of days. In such situations, you have essentially three choices:

If it's a cause that you would normally support with more advanced notice and you can easily accommodate the request, by all means go ahead and give them what you can. Be sure to explain your normal procedure of needing the request far in advance of the event—one month, three months, or whatever timeframe works for you.

If the organization is requesting a large donation or it is a cause that you would normally consider cautiously, then explain your policy and stand firm. Once you do this, however, you can't make any exceptions. Someone will inevitably find out if you let another organization squeeze by, and they will not be speaking kindly of you.

Be sure to get all requests in writing. It's easy to forget what you gave to which organization. Without a written record, you may find that your budget is off, and you won't remember to get records for tax purposes.

Now, you probably think that no one would make a request without having it in writing. I have found that, frequently, people approached us for school and church events with not only no request in writing but not enough information for us to make a reasonable and appropriate business decision.

In order to make a good decision, I recommend actually having a small form to attach to the request before you file it in your tickler for review. (A sample form is included in the Appendix.)

Here is some of the information that is important to obtain:

Name of the organization and contact

Is the contact person the volunteer who has made the request or another person more easily accessible should you have questions? You don't want to bother a volunteer at home who may have just been dropping off requests at various businesses. It will waste time for both of you.

Reason for request

You can make this a quick note such as annual fundraiser, silent auction, benefit for new mammography unit, etc. This will allow you to quickly see if it goes along with your mission, which you have already established.

Deadline

How much lag time do you have? You shouldn't typically be rushed to decide. Just make sure the request is dated when you receive it.

Proof of 501(c)(3) and, if warranted, proof of state sales tax exemption

Remember that you will need these documents for your taxes. The person dropping off the request or mailing it may not include these documents. If that's the case, call and get copies of the documents prior to making a decision.

Contrary to what some believe, all nonprofits are not exempt from paying sales tax. I have been burned by this as have many other businesses donating to charities. Frequently, in the case of small charities, they aren't aware of the difference, especially at the volunteer level. If they refuse to provide the paperwork for you, file the request in the circular file under your desk!

What exactly are they asking for?

Do they want money, a gift certificate for their silent auction, merchandise? We were usually willing to help the person who said, "We'd love this item, but we'd be thrilled with anything you can spare for our auction."

What recognition will you get for your contribution?

Be specific about this. Once I donated a large gift certificate to a silent auction, which I then attended. Imagine my surprise when I didn't see our gift certificate. I approached the organizer who informed me that it had been included in a large "crafts for kids" basket along with gift certificates from my competitors! Not only that, but the only person who would know that I donated was the person who bought the basket. It got my name out to no one else at the auction!

How did they decide to contact you?

Were you just a business in the assigned geographical area to be approached? Are people from the organization regular customers of yours? Are you simply on a mailing list?

When you have far more requests than you have money, service, or merchandise to give, the answer to this question is often a deciding factor. Most people, myself included, are more likely to make a contribution to a regular customer's organization than someone who came into their business not even knowing what the business was exactly, but wanting a contribution.

DECISION TIME

Now that you have all of the information, it's time to make your decision. Clearly, you may have to narrow down and deny some worthy causes, which no one likes to do. Two businesses that I spoke to had a flat policy to avoid this: one honored any request under $50, the other, if it wasn't one of their regularly supported charities, gave a $10 gift certificate.

If you want to donate something to everyone, remember that a gift certificate has a retail value to the recipient but is only costing you the amount you paid wholesale. So, if you give someone a $50 gift certificate and they purchase a blouse from your boutique, they have received an item valued at $50. This is what it would cost them if they came in and purchased it. However, you may have only paid $22 for that blouse. In this situation, it actually costs you $22 as opposed to $50.

Often, the gift certificate is the way to go if you are unable to contribute in the manner that you've been asked. Obviously, if you received a capital campaign letter from your local hospital's development office or another such agency, a gift certificate isn't an option. However, in this case, when you send your response suggest that they contact you for their next fundraiser since you are happy to donate a gift certificate for a service or product.

Remember to think creatively. Let's say you own a printing business. You really would like to support the local high school band's trip to Italy for the international championship, but money is really tight this time of year. You might want to contact the organizer of the particular fundraising event and let him or her know that you'd be happy to donate the printing services for all of their flyers if they are willing to use a stock paper that you have an excess of and allow you to print at the bottom, "Printing courtesy of ABC Printing."

Even though they came to you asking every local business for $200, they may love receiving this service instead. Otherwise, it would have surely cost them much more than $200 for their printing. Not only will you keep the cash, but also you will have used up some of your yellow stock paper, and anyone who gets a flyer will be aware of your generous donation.

Another way you can help with no cost to you is to offer to display flyers. If it's an organization that you believe in, you may even offer to include a blurb in your newsletter or on your Web site. While the organization came to you hoping to elicit a monetary gift, they may be thrilled with what you offer.

If you put information in your business, newsletter, or on your Web site, the organization has the opportunity to not only reach more people but to add more information than a thirty-second pitch allows. Your customers will know that you support this organization. Likewise, any of the organization's supporters that have been referred to your Web site or newsletter will know that the charity has a good relationship with your business.

SAYING NO

From time to time, you may decide that you simply have to deny a request. There are certainly a variety of reasons for this. Perhaps you have already given to this particular group three different times this year. Maybe this month you have had an abundance of requests and, by process of elimination, you are unable to accommodate this organization at this time.

What are the ramifications going to be of saying no? Well, it depends on several factors: how you convey the "no," how strongly the person asking feels about the organization, and what your policies are.

What's the best way to convey the rejection? This can be tricky. You could have a simple form letter that simply states a generic rejection that will apply to any organization that solicits a donation. (See the Appendix.) A form letter such as this is gracious and unoffending, but rather impersonal. I have sent this type of letter to various organizations that contacted me via solicitation letter or an unknown person dropping off a letter at my business, but I never sent one to a regular customer.

You could use a form letter with a check off system listing several of the most common reasons for rejecting a charity's proposal (e.g., not enough notice, doesn't fall within your guidelines for charitable giving). This allows you to check the reasons that pertain to each situation.

The best delivery is to write a short but personal letter. You can give one of a variety of reasonable responses that will say "no" without causing any hard feelings. Remember that small charitable organizations are frequently started for very passionate and often personal reasons, so a rejection can be taken very personally.

In your rejection letter, always express how worthy their organization is and how you certainly wish you could support it. Follow these statements by giving the reason you are unable to support them. If it is an annual cause that you are turning down now but you might like to support in the future, invite them to resubmit next year.

Be sure to close by wishing them well in their endeavors. As someone who has solicited before, I know how hard it is to ask for a donation of product or money. I also know what a difference it is to hear a flat "no" versus a "sorry, we can't, but good luck."

If the request has been made by a customer or an organization you feel particularly close to, you may want to contact them in person or by phone. You can then assure them that you truly wish that you could have offered support and explain exactly why you can't. Most people will understand that you have been inundated with requests or that business has been slow. In fact, most people have been there themselves and will appreciate the extra effort you made in contacting them personally.

BUSINESS PROFILE

FEMAIL CREATIONS
Las Vegas, NV • 800-996-9223 • www.femailcreations.com
Owner: Lisa Hammond • Business: art and gift catalogue

Six years ago while ordering from catalogs, Lisa wished that a woman-owned gift catalog would appear at her doorstep so that she could show her support with her shopping dollars.

Well, today that catalog can appear at your door thanks to Lisa who decided to go for it and start her own catalog business. Femail Creations features handmade works by female artists.

The catalog is issued five times a year and each catalog features a different charity that benefits from the purchase of an item. While each charity is different, most support women, children, or the environment.

Femail Creations has been featured in Oprah's O magazine, and Lisa has been named the Small Business Person of the Year in Las Vegas, Nevada. Her belief is simple: as your business grows so does your ability to give back. This is how she runs her business.

I discovered Femail Creations a few years ago when a catalog arrived. Her Web site is a must to visit as an example of effective and admirable cause-related marketing.

CHARITY PROFILE

WOMEN'S CAREER CLOTHING CLOSET
219 Walnut Street • Morgantown, WV 26505 • 304-296-0221
jeddog@adelpha.net • Contact: Sabrina Bindocci

MISSION: To facilitate upward mobility for underprivileged women by providing professional clothing and job training referrals free of charge.

The Woman's Career Clothing Closet was founded to help increase employment opportunities. By offering their services, one immediate need of women transferring from welfare to work is met. The confidence a woman feels at being appropriately outfitted reflects well in her presentation.

While there are organizations around the country that provide the first interview outfit, this organization happily provides a complete outfit including accessories once a month.

Besides clothing, educational and computer training referrals are offered, as well as job interviewing skills and etiquette. Women's health information is also offered. Since opening in 1998 more than 300 women have been helped.

This organization would be an ideal type of organization for a beauty salon or business consultant to partner with.

CHAPTER 8

Effects of Outside Influences

Why is a cause-related marketing campaign by a small community business so important in today's world? There are several reasons: the financial climate of the country is not at its best; unemployment rates are up; the nation has been rocked by scandal; and, of course, we are still recovering from the September 11 attacks. All of these outside influences have a direct and profound impact on both small businesses and small community nonprofits.

THE CURRENT ECONOMY

First, it was Enron, then Arthur Anderson and WorldCom and then questions surrounding Martha Stewart. The stock market is plummeting, and people are becoming frightened about their futures. How and when will they retire? How will they pay for their children's educations? How safe are their jobs?

There is some speculation that this may cause charitable giving to suffer. This makes cause-related marketing efforts even more appealing to the consumer.

While we may be watching our spending and closing our checkbooks to capital campaign donations, we still will be making some purchases. If we're purchasing flowers for the holidays, a gift, or wedding and florist A and florist B are about the same price, but florist B donates ten percent of profits to a local shelter, it makes great sense to purchase from them and help a cause at the same time.

The economy also affects charitable giving by altering the grants that foundations award. Most nonprofit foundations that award grants do so by using the interest from their investments. The volatility of the current market has the potential to directly affect how much interest is available to give.

EMPLOYMENT CONCERNS

With all of the scandal buzzing about large, well-respected corporations and their less than honorable business practices, people are left wondering which company will be next. Each time the shoe drops and a bankruptcy is filed, there are mass layoffs at all levels and many employees lose huge amounts of money from company investments. Many of these companies also had a foundation arm for community giving that is now crippled. Being laid off or the fear of "being next" can understandably put any nonessential spending on the back burner if it's not eliminated altogether. This includes charitable giving.

POST SEPTEMBER 11

Immediately following the attack on September 11, people raced to donate to help the victims, their families, and the rescue workers. People volunteered, wrote checks—whatever they could do to help. Large charitable organizations quickly set up special arms of their organizations just for gifts for September 11. Community and special interest groups formed nonprofit charitable organizations for a specific cause, such as families of a particular rescue unit.

So many nonprofits related to this tragedy were formed that the IRS lists them in a separate section on their nonprofit list. According to the Better Business Bureau, there were over 200 new organizations in New York State alone.

The October 15, 2001 edition of *The NonProfit Times Financial Management Edition*, reported that "giving to non-relief organizations took a major hit in the weeks immediately following the attack." The same article cites a study by the Center on Philanthropy for the American Association of Fundraising Council Trust for Philanthropy that examined the economic and giving changes surrounding thirteen major events of terrorism, acts of war, and political or economic crises. The study showed mostly positive giving numbers the year before, the year of, and year after such events.

Two studies were done showing positive responses to charitable giving. The first, a poll released by Independent Sector shows the following:

- Seventy percent of Americans reported some form of charitable involvement in response to September 11. (This includes blood donation and volunteering as well as financial gifts.)

- Fifty-eight percent gave a financial contribution.

- Seventy-three percent of September 11 givers say they will continue to give as much or more than they usually give to other charities.

- Fifty percent of Americans say an economic slow-down will reduce giving.

- Five percent reported giving over the Internet.

While this report looks quite good for nonprofits overall, several small community charities have discussed a drop-off in some donations and grants being awarded. This provides a great opportunity for you to work with your community nonprofits.

It is also clear that since September 11 people are more concerned about the social awareness of businesses and expect them to participate in charitable works. This is evident through a poll released by Cone/Roper in November 2001. It reports that eight in ten Americans (seventy-nine percent) believe that companies have a responsibility to support causes. This is up from sixty-five percent in March 2001. Almost nine in ten Americans (eighty eight percent) feel that during an economic downturn it is even more important for businesses to continue supporting causes. This is up from seventy-one percent in March 2001.

All of the above information just reiterates the importance of a cause-related marketing campaign and how it can benefit both your business and small charities.

THE UP SIDE FOR THE SMALL BUSINESS

How can there be an upside you ask? The small business appears to be suffering more than ever in recent history.

I agree—it's a tough time. But that's what gives you an edge. There are times when we still want and need both tangible goods and services, but we still want to help.

In fact, I recently spoke to Joanna Dreifus, who operates the website www.marriedforgood.com and is on the board of www.idofoundation.com.

When I happened across these sites, I was naturally intrigued. They were started by Joanna when she was getting married. Wanting to help others, Joanna and her husband, Sandy, decided that, rather than spend the money for table favors, they would donate to The Hospital for Special Surgery since Joanna had been a patient there as a teenager. They also donated to The Blue Card, a New York charity that helps needy Holocaust survivors. On each table they placed a card explaining the organizations to which they had made donations.

Joanna's Web site contains many more stories about philanthropic couples. The mission of the site is to increase visibility and donations to charities, as well as to encourage occasion-based giving.

This is a great example of opportunities for businesses. Suppose you are a printer. You might offer to donate a percentage of the cost of the couple's invitations to the charity of their choice.

Or, maybe you want to take it a step further and not only give a percentage to the charity, but add a discount to the couple in return for a statement in small print on the back of invitations or programs saying something like, "Printed by B.J. Printing, who donated a portion of their profits to Sally and Bob's selected charity, Baby Doe Foundation." This gives both you and the charity greater exposure.

So while today's environment seems a bit shaky, cause-related marketing endeavors can truly turn lemons into lemonade for small businesses, community nonprofit organizations, and the buying public. What more could we ask for?

BUSINESS PROFILE

BROWN & COMPANY GRAPHIC DESIGNS
801 Islington Street, Suite 35 • Portsmouth, NH 03801
603-436-5239 • www.browndesign.com
Owner: Mary Jo Brown • Business: Graphic Design

Mary Jo Brown began Brown & Company eleven years ago. Believing from the beginning that she had a responsibility to give back to her community, she found it easy to say yes to nonprofits. It didn't take long for her to discover that there is a large, worthwhile nonprofit community out there, and that she would have to come up with a way to manage requests more efficiently.

Her staff suggested they develop a pro bono partnership model, which has served well her company and many nonprofits. In this model, the nonprofit organization submits an application. The Brown staff evaluates the applicants, narrows them down to five, and then asks those finalists to make a presentation to the company. The presentations not only allow the nonprofits to express their missions and needs, but also allow the staff to learn more about a worthy organization, which has resulted in many individual volunteer opportunities as well.

Finally, the staff votes, and the partner is chosen. Brown & Company then donates 200 hours of service to their partner. Pro bono partnerships last for one year. The nonprofits that were not chosen are invited to reapply the following year.

I found Mary Jo through the Giving New England organization. The application for the pro bono partnership is on the Web site, and Mary Jo encourages you to use a part or all of it for your business.

CHARITY PROFILE

ADVOCATES FOR BLIND CHILDREN INTERNATIONAL
3500 W. Parmer Lane • Austin, TX 78727
512-218-8110 • timtutt@att.net • Web site coming soon
Contact: Steven Foreman

MISSION: To assist blind and vision impaired children around the world by providing education, financial assistance, and advocacy. ABCI seeks to serve as a link between Western Resources and other-world needs.

When Steven Foreman read a story in a news magazine about a blind child in war-torn Bosnia, he felt the need to help. As someone with many years of experience teaching visually impaired and blind children and adults to use a white cane, Steven realized that he possessed a skill sorely needed in a war-torn area.

While many blind and visually impaired people are able to maneuver quite well by memorizing their surroundings—the drug store is 6 paces out of my door and 12 paces to the left—this would no longer be possible for those now stepping onto rubble. Due to the war, many things no longer existed and those that did were no longer easily accessible. Beyond this, it would be impossible for the blind person to see and recognize danger, such as land mines.

After working with the Missions Agencies of The Christian Church (Disciples of Christ) and International relief personnel, Steven was able to make contact with

The School for the Blind in Sarajevo. Using his life savings, he traveled there several times during the next three years.

Wanting to do more and realizing the limitations both physically and financially, Steven, along with others committed to the cause, started a nonprofit organization run solely by volunteers.

Their future hopes are to be able to send teams in to wartorn areas to not just teach white cane usage to those in need, but to train others so that the training will not stop when ABCI teams leave. One hundred percent of money donated to the organization is used for ABCI programs.

BIBLIOGRAPHY

Articles / Studies

Cone, C. Cause Branding in the 21st Century. Accessed at www.psaresearch.com.

Staff. Good Deeds Attract Customers and Workers (survey results on public opinion on corporate social activity), *USA Today* Magazine (August 1999). Accessed at www.usaweekend.com.

Williams-Harold, B. Spending With Heart. Blackenterprise.com (July 1998).

Chan, A.; Lawrence, M. Post –September 11th: Major Shift in American Attitudes Towards Companies Involved With Social Issues, press release (November 11, 2001).

Carpenter, C.; Clolery, P. Non-Relief Fundraising Sputtering in Wake of Attacks. *The Non Profit Times.* (October 15, 2001).

Independent Sector. Charitable Giving: September 11th and Beyond, Independent Sector Survey, press release (October 23, 2001).

Kansas Attorney General's office. Charities: Giving Wisely. Accessed at www.ink.org/ksag/contents/consumer/charity.htm.

Cohen, R. Post 9/11 Considerations and Agendas for Funders and Fundraisers. *Nonprofit Quarterly.* October 2001.

Promotion Marketing Association and Gable Group. Integration of Internet Marketing Will be Next Major Trend. PR Newswire Survey (May 30, 2000).

Chan, A.; Lawrence, M. Americans Define "What's Right" for Companies in Response to Terrorist Attack, national poll by Cone Research (September 27, 2001).

Chan, A.; Lawrence, M; DaSilva, A. Post-September 11th: Major Shift in American Attitudes Towards Companies Involved With Social Issues, Cone/Roper corporate citizenship study. (November 11, 2001).

McCall, K. Cause and Effect—Have You Ever Heard of Cause-related Marketing? Maybe It's Time You Looked Into It. *Entrepreneur's Start-Ups* Magazine. (November 2000).

Web sites

www.irs.gov

www.charitywatch.org

www.give.org

www.nptimes.com

www.coneinc.com

www.nonprofit.about.com

www.independentsector.com

www.entrepreneur.com

APPENDIX

Getting Started Worksheet

Taking a few minutes to fill out this simple worksheet (referenced in Chapter 2) may help you narrow your focus and choose your charities wisely.

What are your interests when not working, such as reading, cooking, hiking, etc?

_____

_____

_____

_____

What types of organizations do you or would you most likely support yourself? (children, medical, homeless, animals, etc)

_____

_____

_____

_____

What kind of customers does your business attract? (children, parents, singles, women, urbanites, outdoorsmen, cooks, etc)

_____

_____

_____

_____

What kind of charities do you believe your customers would be inclined to support? (If you are a hunting store, it is unlikely that PETA supporters would be your customers. If you cater to upper class business women, they may very well be inclined to support organizations that benefit women.)

_____

_____

_____

_____

Now look at your answers and see if there are commonalities.

Here are a couple of examples of reviewing answers and choosing a cause.

Example 1

Your passion is cooking, you support children's charities, your customer demographics are mostly women who you believe would support children's causes, and your business is a gift shop.

Yours is a pretty easy decision since interests are similar and most people are interested in helping children. With your interest in cooking you could partner with a local food bank, an organization that provides for homeless children, or an organization that teaches children about good nutrition.

Example 2

You love the outdoors, hiking, and gardening. In fact, you love all things natural, including natural remedies. You are skeptical of physicians and traditional medicine in general, you only use homeopathic remedies and would never consider using something like chemotherapy.

You run a temporary worker service. This means that your customers potentially run the gamut of very conservative to ultra liberal and may include physicians, pharmacies, or other similar businesses. In order to avoid any controversy, it might not be in your business' best interest to partner with an organization supporting an alternative medical practice that condemns the use of traditional treatment. Even if your clientele is not in the medical field, this is a hot and controversial topic, and your client may not want their dollars to go to support your cause.

In such a case you will have to make a tough decision: Am I going to partner with an organization that I believe in personally, or is this a marketing decision where I consider my customers' opinions as well?

Sample Form for Considering Requests

Charity request: _____

_____

Date received: _____

Received from (*person/organization/contact number*): ____

_____

_____

How did they hear about us: _____

_____

_____

Reason for request: _____

_____

_____

_____

Donation deadline: _____

Monetary or other: _____

_____

Proof of 501(c)(3): *should be attached*

Proof of State Tax Exemption: *should be attached*

Have we contributed before (if yes, when) _____

_____

_____

Decision: _____

_____

Reason: _____

_____

_____

_____

_____

If yes, gift (if monetary, list amount given): _____

_____

Be sure to keep this on file for future reference. A copy should also go to your accountant.

Turning Down a Donation Request

Turning down a worthwhile organization is always a difficult thing to have to do. Unfortunately, it is sometimes necessary. As mentioned in Chapter 7, here are a couple of ways that it can be done graciously.

Sample 1

Form Letter—Although saying no, the charity will have an idea as to your reasons, as well as knowing if you are a "fit" for their next event.

Dear Mr. Jackson,

Thank you for thinking of us when organizing your event. While we feel very supportive of your organization, we are unable to donate at this time for the following reason(s):

____ The organization does not fall into our current cause mission statement. We support only those organizations which benefit the environment.

____ The request arrived past the deadline for consideration. All requests must be received at least three months prior to the event.

____ Our philanthropic budget will not allow a contribution at this time.

We wish you much success with your endeavors and encourage you to contact us for support at another time.

Sincerely,
Jane Doe, Owner, Jane's Landscaping Service

Sample 2

Standard letter—While this may seem a bit cold and callous, you may find it appropriate in some cases. If you are working in a very busy and understaffed business, you may simply not have the time to respond individually to all of your requests. This generic response is certainly more courteous than simply ignoring the request altogether.

Dear Ms. Caffrey,

Thank you for contacting us recently concerning a contribution. While your organization is clearly worthwhile, we are unable to contribute at this time.

We certainly wish you well and would encourage you to contact us again in the future.

Sincerely,
John Smith, Owner, Smith and Associates

Sample 3

Personal Note—This can be very short and informal, but the requester will know that, although you can't give now, you do really care about the organization and/or event.

Dear Susan,

While we would love to be able to contribute to your run next month, it is simply not feasible at this time. We wish that we had been aware of your event earlier. If this is an annual event please contact us four to six months ahead of time so that we can put you on the calendar.

Although we are unable to make a donation, we would be very happy to allow you to hang a poster or distribute flyers in our business. [*This depends on your type of business.*]

[*Optional— if you would like to donate an item, include a statement similar to the following.*] While not a monetary gift, we would be more than happy to offer coupons for your runners' bags or gift certificates for winners.

We look forward to hearing from you in the future.

Sincerely,
Kate Jones, Owner, Kate's Cafe

Press Releases

Bad Example

Please print this.

Feel like you have to stay at home on Cupid's Day due to dietary restrictions? Not this year.

Jane Smart will make selections for two separate four-course meals—one for those choosing a heart healthy menu and another for those who require a diabetic meal. Chef/owner Ron Hub will be working closely with Smart to make the selections sumptuous.

Hub is committed to providing tasty and healthy meals.

To make reservations for Valentine's Day, call 213-222-4321. Smart is available to speak at your civic clubs and also provides individual counseling. She can be reached at 213-321-4534.

Anyone wanting more information on how to get involved with a local chapter of the American Heart Association should call 213-451-9000.

There are several very basic and frequent mistakes in this example. See if you can find them, then check the list below.

- *It is not marked clearly that this is a press release nor is it addressed to a specific person at the publication.*

- *It reads almost like an advertisement—there is no mention of a donation or teaming with the Heart Association. Just a number for the Heart Association at the end.*

- *Jane Smart is not properly identified. What are her qualifications to select menus or speak to civic organizations? What kind of counseling does she provide?*

- *Although the chef's name is mentioned, the name of his restaurant is not.*

- *While it is clear from the content that this event is February 14, this will not always be the case. It is very important to always put a date in the heading.*

- *Finally, there is no contact information. You may think that this is not an important detail since there are several phone numbers already included in the text. However, a reporter isn't going to start calling numbers from the body of the release hoping to reach the appropriate person. A name and contact phone number should always be listed at the top of a release.*

These are all very frequently made mistakes and even one can keep your press release out of the paper.

Good Example

February 5, 2002

For Immediate Release [*or a particular date or time frame can be placed here*]

Contact: Jane Smart at 213-321-4534

Healthy and Romantic Dining for Valentine's Day

Feel like you have to stay at home on Cupid's Day due to dietary restrictions? Not this year.

Jane Smart, a registered dietitian and personal nutrition consultant, has teamed with Brownville's chapter of the American Heart Association.

Smart will make selections for two separate four-course meals—one for those choosing a heart healthy menu and another for those who require a diabetic meal. Brownville Inn's chef/owner Ron Hub will be working closely with Smart to make the selections sumptuous.

Hub is committed to providing tasty and healthy meals and will donate fifty percent of the Valentine's Day meal proceeds to the local chapter of the American Heart Association.

To make reservations for Valentine's Day, call Brownville Inn at 213-222-4321. Smart is available to speak at your civic clubs and also provides individual nutrition counseling. She can be reached at 213-321-4534.

Anyone wanting more information on how to get involved with a local chapter of the American Heart Association should call 213-451-9000.

Resources

Books

Steckel, Richard, Robin Simmons, Jeffrey Simmons, and Norman Tanen. *Making Money While Making a Difference.* Homewood, Illinois. High Tide Press. 1999.

Austin, James E. *The Collaboration Challenge: How Nonprofits and Busiensses Succeed Through Strategic Alliances.* San Francisco, California. Jossey-Bass. 2000.

Michaels, Nancy, and Debbi J. Karpowicz. *Off-The-Wall Marketing Ideas.* Avon, Massachusetts. Adams Media Corporation. 2000.

Web sites

Better Business Bureau for nonprofits: www.give.org

Website for American Institute of Philanthropy: a charity watchdog organization. www.charitywatch.org

Internal Revenue Service: www.irs.org

Non Profit Times Web site: a newsletter with great articles concerning nonprofits. www.nptimes.com

Independent Sector: Web site for coalition of nonprofits. www.independentsector.org

The Community Foundation: Web site for the Boulder, Colorado, area that has excellent information relevant to business owners in all regions. www.commfound.org

Giving New England: Web site of organized philanthropy throughout New England. This site has a tremendous amount of information and ideas.
www.givenewengland.org

Community Partnerships With Youth, Inc.: a national training and development program to promote young philanthropists ages 7-11. www.cpyinc.org

Married For Good: a great Web site that shows how to incorporate charity into your wedding and highlights several who have. This could inspire businesses who deal with weddings to join forces with the couple to help a charity while doing their job. www.marriedforgood.com

There are many, many more wonderful Web sites to check out for ideas and inspiration. I encourage you to do a search on cause-related marketing and research some more ideas.

Design Services

Vince Stavrowsky, Shell Media
vinces@shellmedia.com

Tamara Dever, TLC Graphics (book design)
tamara@tlcgraphics.com
www.TLCGraphics.com

Theresa Stachowiak, Stellular Design
stellular@ptd.net
www.stellulardesign.com

Teaching Children and Teens

A sense of giving and community stewardship is not limited to adults. In fact, Community Partnerships with Youth, Inc., a nonprofit organization, offers training and curriculum for programs beginning at the age of five.

According to their mission statement, they exist to assist young people, ages five to eighteen years, to understand the history, philosophy, and the acts of philanthropy (giving and serving) which will instill in them the conviction to plan for themselves a lifetime commitment to serve.

CPY, Inc. has developed several curriculum including "The Word for Me is PHILANTHROPY" and "Youth as Philanthropists." Additionally, Janet Wakefield, Executive Director, is the author of, *What if Everybody Gave?*, a children's storybook.

Training is available nationwide through CPY, Inc.

For additional information contact:

Janet Wakefield, Executive Director
Lydi Davidson, Assistant Director
Community Partnerships With Youth, Inc.
556 East Jefferson St., Suite 306
Franklin, Indiana 46131
317-736-7947
www.cpyinc.org

Youth Nonprofit Organization

A youth civic organization can be a great one to partner with and/or support. Here is an example of one that, although under the umbrella of a national organization, has chapters that are run independently and can be found in most communities.

Interact Club
Sponsored by local Rotary Clubs
(contact your local club)
www.rotary.org

Interact Club is a high school service club that falls under the umbrella of Rotary, International. Each Interact is sponsored by a local Rotary Club. The Rotary Club provides a liaison, and a teacher at the local high school commits to being the director.

Clubs decide their own service projects and frequently work together with the local Rotary Club on various projects.

I am the liaison for our club, and I am constantly amazed at the commitment the kids have and what great service projects they undertake, from putting together shoeboxes of items for residents at nursing homes to cleaning up community parks.

State Agencies That Oversee
Charitable Organizations

The following links will take you to the agencies in all states that govern charitable organizations. If you have any concerns or questions about a charity, don't hesitate to contact the following agencies for information. At the time of publication the following information was correct, but offices do occasionally change—sometimes as soon as new officials are elected. If a link provided here doesn't work, you can go to the state's home page (usually www.state.ca.us, inserting your state's abbreviation between "state" and "us") and search for "charitable organizations."

Alabama: Office of the Attorney General
www.ago.state.al.us/consumer_charities.cfm

Alaska: The Consumer Protection Unit
www.law.state.ak.us/consumer/index.html

Arizona: Office of the Secretary of State
www.sosaz.com/Business_Services/Charities.htm

Arkansas: Office of the Attorney General
www.ag.state.ar.us/

California: Office of the Attorney General
http://caag.state.ca.us/charities

Colorado: Office of the Attorney General
www.ago.state.co.us/consprot/statutes/charity.htm

Connecticut: Office of the Attorney General
www.cslib.org/attygenl/mainlinks/tabindex8.htm

Delaware: Office of the Attorney General
www.state.de.us/attgen

District of Columbia: Department of Consumer and
Regulatory Affairs
dcra.dc.gov/main.shtm

Florida: Division of Consumer Services
www.800helpfla.com/~cs/gift_givers/search.html

Georgia: Office of the Secretary of State
www.sos.state.ga.us/securities/charitysearch.htm

Hawaii: Office of Consumer Protection
www.hawaii.gov/

Idaho: Office of the Attorney General
www.state.id.us/ag (to file a complaint only)

Illinois: Office of the Attorney General
www.ag.state.il.us/charitable/charity.html

Indiana: Office of the Attorney General
www.state.in.us/attorneygeneral/

Iowa: Office of the Attorney General
www.state.ia.us/government/ag/charity1.htm

Kansas: Office of the Secretary of State
www.kssos.org/charity.html

Kentucky: Office of the Attorney General
www.law.state.ky.us/cp/charity.htm

Louisiana: Office of the Attorney General
www.ag.state.la.us

Maine: Office of the Attorney General
www.state.me.us/ag

Maryland: Office of the Secretary of State
www.sos.state.md.us/sos/charity/html/cod.html

Massachusetts: Office of the Attorney General
www.ago.state.ma.us

Michigan: Office of the Attorney General
www.ag.state.mi.us/charities/charities.htm

Minnesota: Office of the Attorney General
www.ag.state.mn.us/charities/Default.htm

Mississippi: Office of the Secretary of State
www.sos.state.ms.us/regenf/charities/charities.asp

Missouri: Office of the Attorney General
www.ago.state.mo.us/complant.htm

Montana: Office of Consumer Affairs
http://discoveringmontana.com/doa/
consumerProtection/Index.htm

Nebraska: Office of the Attorney General
www.ago.state.ne.us

Nevada: Consumer Affairs Division
www.fyiconsumer.org

New Hampshire: Department of Justice
www.state.nh.us/nhdoj/CHARITABLE/char.html

New Jersey: Office of Consumer Protection
www.state.nj.us/lps/ca/ocp.htm#charity

New Mexico: Office of the Attorney General
www.ago.state.nm.us/Protection/
consumer_protection.html

New York: Office of the Attorney General
www.oag.state.ny.us/charities/charities.html

North Carolina: Office of the Secretary of State
www.secretary.state.nc.us/csl/index.html

North Dakota: Office of the Attorney General
www.ag.state.nd.us/ (information on charities in PDF
format)

Ohio: Office of the Attorney General
www.ag.state.oh.us/default

Oklahoma: Office of the Attorney General
www.oag.state.ok.us

Oregon: Office of the Attorney General
www.doj.state.or.us/ChariGroup/welcome2.htm

Pennsylvania: Department of State
www.dos.state.pa.us/char/site/default.asp

Rhode Island: Department of Business Regulation
www.dbr.state.ri.us/char_orgs.html

South Carolina: Office of the Secretary of State
www.scsos.com/charities.htm

South Dakota: Office of the Attorney General
www.state.sd.us/attorney/divisions/consumer/
index.htm

Tennessee: Department of State
www.state.tn.us/sos/charity.htm

Texas: Office of the Attorney General
www.oag.state.tx.us/website/sitetoc.htm

Utah: Division of Consumer Protection
www.commerce.utah.gov/dcp/index.html

Vermont: Office of the Attorney General
www.state.vt.us/atg/charity%20information.htm

Virginia: Office of Consumer Affairs
www.vdacs.state.va.us/index.html

Washington: Office of the Secretary of State
www.secstate.wa.gov/charities/default.htm

West Virginia: Office of the Secretary of State
www.wvsos.com

Wisconsin: Department of Regulation and Licensing
www.drl.state.wi.us

Wyoming: Office of the Secretary of State
http://soswy.state.wy.us/index_1.htm

ABOUT THE AUTHOR

Peggy Linial spent years in the healthcare field, first in a clinical capacity where she was director of cardiology, ran a support group for heart patients, and wrote patient education materials. She then spent twelve years in EMS textbook publishing, lecturing frequently around the country.

After leaving healthcare, Peggy opened a retail business. During this time she appeared frequently on local and national television and in the news as a result of her cause-related marketing activities.

Peggy is currently a columnist for the *Round Rock Leader*, a newspaper in Round Rock, Texas, and a judge for the national Benjamin Franklin Awards. Peggy teaches classes in cause-related marketing at the University of Texas. She is active in and serves on the board of the Rotary Club.

Peggy lives in Texas with her husband, George, and their two golden retrievers, Sammi and Misha.